OUR COMMONS: POLITICAL IDEAS FOR A NEW EUROPE

Edited by Sophie Bloemen and
Thomas de Groot

Colophon

Our Commons: Political Ideas for a New Europe
Editors: Sophie Bloemen and Thomas de Groot

Authors: Kate Raworth, George Monbiot, David Hammerstein, Cecile Blanchet, Jose Louis Vivero Pol, Christian Iaione, Sheila Foster, Doina Petrescu, Constantin Petcou, Trebor Scholz, May Ishikawa Sutton, Ellen 't Hoen, Jean-Francois Alesandrini, Benjamin Coriat, Michel Bauwens, Silke Helfrich, David Bollier, Thomas de Groot and Sophie Bloemen.

Copy-editor: Mai Ishikawa Sutton

Cover art and illustrations: Mercė M. Tarrės/Guerilla Media Collective

Typesetting: Donato Spinelli

Production: Sepp Eckenhaussen and Donato Spinelli

Published by the Institute of Network Cultures, Amsterdam, 2019.

ISBN 978-94-92302-35-9

Contact
Commons Network
Keizersgracht 102, 1015CV, Amsterdam, The Netherlands

Email: info@commonsnetwork.eu

Web: http://www.commonsnetwork.org

Preface

Our world is darkening and major shifts are coming. Our social and economic systems are strained and we have reached the limits of what the planet can endure. We are yearning for change, but what does that look like and where do we go from there?

We believe real change happens when we challenge the status quo and embrace the future. The commons help us do both. In this book, we have tried to showcase how powerful that combination can be.

This book would not have been possible without the support of the Fondation Charles Léopold Mayer pour le Progrès de l'Homme. We also could not have done any of this without the work of our partners, teachers and friends in the international commons movement.

Thomas and Sophie, Amsterdam, April 2019.

Table of Contents

1. INTRODUCTION: SHIFTING PARADIGMS

Thomas de Groot and Sophie Bloemen

Introduction: Shifting Paradigms

by Thomas de Groot and Sophie Bloemen

'Europe' is more an idea than a geographical unit. In many ways, it remains a promise, something that one day might take shape. How we design that promise is continuously up for debate. The current dominant shape of the idea that we call Europe is simply not good enough. We must reinvigorate its promise.

Our Europe is optimistic, driven by ideas and stories that have the common good in mind. Our Europe is inspired by human flourishing and mutual trust. Our Europe is built on generosity and hope, not on extraction and dogma. It is built on communities and citizens, not on markets and consumers.

The foundational stories of collective post-war reconstruction and the mantra of 'never again' have lost their appeal. Europe is now facing various forms of social and political regression, notably the rise of new forms of nationalist, neo-fascist and undemocratic movements.

Europe needs new stories that orient us towards a brighter future. We believe that one of these stories is that of the commons. It is the story of people jointly stewarding resources, like water or energy or even cities and knowledge. It is a story of communities, of collaborative and democratic practices. The commons have been a forgotten sector of our society and our economy. They convey the space in which communities write their own rules. The commons presuppose activity, communication and democratic stewardship. They move us away from linear thinking and individualism, towards ecosystems and social relationships.

Perceiving our shared resources — like water, land, air, cultural heritage and scientific achievements — as global commons inspires us to take a certain ethical perspective. It leads us to recognize the imperative to jointly and equitably govern these resources, in a way that maintains the wealth of our planet. It implies a regenerative economy that sustains the planet, not an extractive one that destroys it. Embracing the commons fosters a culture of reciprocity to bring about a more socially and ecologically sustainable society.

Commons Network has in the last several years worked to tell that story, to convey the logic of the commons in policy circles, in civil society and in the public debate. Together with others, we saw the enormous power and potential of this story and practice, the collective potential of all commoners. We have acted as a think tank, as organisers, as activists and advocates. We published papers, wrote articles, organised Assemblies, met countless people and learned about thousands of initiatives. We saw how the commons connects struggles in different realms and bridges movements and approaches: it provides a new vocabulary for social justice and collective action for a social-ecological transition.

This renewed claim to community, belonging and collaborative values makes a new politics and a new economy possible. Yes, we argue that this vision brings us closer to the ideal of Europe as a post-nationalist space.1 Through trans-local solidarity and multilayered belonging, we can escape the stand-off between detached cosmopolitanism and regressive nationalism.

Having learned about the different practices and forms of commons and what they need from institutions to thrive, we decided to bring it all together. Here, we showcase the ideas, the people, the practices and the policy implications. This book offers an insight into this growing movement. While we are writing this, new commons initiatives are emerging, adding to the theories and practies and further developing the discourse.

Working on the commons, we have come to observe transformative ideas emerging all around us. More and more people dare to imagine radically different futures, beyond 'there is no alternative'. More and more policymakers are adopting new concepts like food sovereignty or 'the Doughnut'. More and more activists are merging anti-racism and eco-feminism in one intersectional and emancipatory theory of change. Even de-growth, a concept that is still too radical for most greens and social-democrats, is slowly becoming more mainstream. We have moved past the neoliberal consensus. We have come to recognize the limits of our planet and the boundaries of the living world as we respect our embedded role in it.

The commons are not primarily a political theory, but first and foremost a practice emerging from the bottom-up. Everywhere, people are engaging in alternative practices as part of the struggle for ecological, social and cultural transition within their communities. Local energy cooperatives are prioritising community wealth and open access medical journals are sharing knowledge – these practices represent social and cultural shifts in value models.

While societal shifts are often framed in terms of economy or technologies, they are rooted in cultural change. Our culture reflects and shapes our values and how we attribute meaning to our lives. Many current community-led and social innovation initiatives contain strong elements of practical cultural change. New social values and practices are enabling communities to be generative instead of extractive. This is creating a new civic and cultural ethic that is breaking with conventional notions of citizenship and participation.

The regeneration activities of commoners showcase, above all, cultural manifestations of new ways of daily life.

The European Union and its member states have a huge role to play in facilitating social and ecological transition. The political project of the European Union could be truly transformative. Yet for now, our institutions are firmly grounded in outdated frames of thinking. Most of the policy that originates in Brussels is based on endless growth, markets and competition. In order to transition to a different economy and society, we must first have a vision. It is crucial that a large transformative vision gains the support of institutions and policymakers.

The commons often emerge from the bottom up; they are dependent on community processes and their logic is mostly at odds with the EU's institutional logic. However, we believe there is an important role for EU politics and policy to create the right incentives, to remove hurdles and to support this re-emerging sector. Supporting communities means addressing the sense of losing control, identity and security. As a post-nationalist project, the EU will, ideally, undergo a change in consciousness away from nationalism, moving toward a flexible mode of citizenship that allows for multiple belongings.

This publication explores these new politics and describes the commons in different spheres of society, economy and politics. With these stories, positions, and visions we aim to inspire but also give clear direction. The book is divided into seven thematic sections. Most sections have a theoretical position and a practical case study. All sections feature influential thinkers whose voices we want to amplify. This book is comprised of the insights of more than 20 writers, activists and pioneers, standing on the shoulders of hundreds more.

Kate Raworth and George Monbiot invited us to Oxford to discuss the role of the commons in their work, which led to the second chapter. In our conversation, George Monbiot addresses the political potential of the commons as a fundamental building block for a new 'politics of belonging'. Kate Raworth explains how the commons can help us arrive at a new, different economy, one that serves people and planet.

In the next chapter, we continue to re-think what aspects of our daily life belong to the domain of the market and the commons. Energy as a commons is presented by Commons Network co-founder David Hammerstein with a clear message: unless we accept de-growth as the only viable path forward, no amount of renewable energy will help us. Cecile Blanchet takes us on a journey to an energy cooperative in chapter 4, setting the scene for a good overview of the current debate on renewables and energy democracy.

In chapter 5, Jose Luis Vivero-Pol offers a passionate plea for food as commons. Food as a system, from farmer to our plate, from the cultural notion of food to its function in our society, should never be a commodity, he argues. In chapter 6, Thomas de Groot investigates how commoners on the ground are bringing this idea to life, in a case study of FoodTopia in Spain and BuurtBuik in The Netherlands.

Urban policies are of critical importance to the emergence of the commons. The groundbreaking work that Sheila Foster and Christian Iaione have done in the emerging field of urban commons gives us tools to do this. In chapter 7, they describe how they arrived at their vision. In chapter 8, Doina Petrescu and Constantin Petcou deliver an urgent appeal to architects to embrace the commons through their case study on R-Urban and 'aaa', a collective of autonomous architects that take the commons as the foundational principle of their work. George Monbiot returns in chapter 9, to tell the story of Barking and Dagenham, one of the only 'Leave-voting' boroughs in the London area. Monbiot convincingly presents this case study as the potential start of a national transformation.

A citizen-based digital sphere that works for people? In chapter 10, Sophie Bloemen, Alek Tarkowski and Paul Keller present their new vision for a digital Europe, built on core principles like decentralisation and digital commons. Democratic ownership is a path forward, away from an economic dead end. That is why, in chapter 11, we asked Trebor Scholz to write about platform cooperatives, which are a good example of democratising the internet. How hard it is to imagine a different internet, one without near-monopolies from SIlicon Valley and surveillance capitalism, is shown by Commons Network fellow Mai Ishikawa Sutton in chapter 12.

As long as we refuse to see biomedical knowledge as a commons, we will never achieve full accessibility to medicines. That is what Sophie Bloemen argues in chapter 13, in her invocation of the commons to bolster the access to medicines movement. How this might work in practice is demonstrated in chapters 14 and 15, where we present the cases of the Drugs for Neglected Diseases Initiative (DNDi) and the Medicines Patent Pool (MPP). Benjamin Coriat and co-authors of DNDi brief us in detail about how a non-profit medicines developer functions as a commons. MPP-founder Ellen 't Hoen gives us a detailed account of the vision and the process that led to the Patent Pool.

Finally, we talk to commons-thinkers Michel Bauwens, Silke Helfrich and David Bollier for an in-depth discussion about the commons movement, what commoners can do for Europe and vice versa.

Our Commons is first released online, as an e-book. In the summer of 2019, the team behind this work will continue the process of organic publication. We will release individual sections as booklets, addressed at different audiences. We will work on a web-version of all the texts, for easier re-use and remixing. We embrace the principle of design global, produce local or in this case, print on demand. Towards the autumn of 2019, we will start the process of translating this work in Dutch, to publish it in traditional book form in The Netherlands. We hope that Our Commons will inspire people to take action.

2. THE POTENTIAL OF THE COMMONS: A CONVERSATION WITH KATE RAWORTH AND GEORGE MONBIOT

Thomas de Groot and Sophie Bloemen

The Potential of the Commons: A Conversation with Kate Raworth and George Monbiot

by Thomas de Groot and Sophie Bloemen

It's hard to overstate the influence Kate Raworth and George Monbiot have had on the increasing popular attention to the commons. Doughnut Economics, the best-selling book that Raworth published in 2017, sent shockwaves through the world of economics and politics.1 Out of the Wreckage, Monbiot's best-selling book from 2017, struck a chord with policymakers and activists.2 More importantly, both writers have managed to reach an audience that goes far beyond academia or policy circles. Their ideas are discussed in mainstream media, from newspapers to talkshows, and they are quoted by politicians and activists. Both have managed to built platforms for themselves that reach milions of people. And both of them discuss the commons at length. We sat down with them in Oxford for a conversation about the problems we face and how the commons can help us make things better.

The Doughnut and the commons

Doughnut Economics, according to some, represents a true paradigm shift in economics. The book fundamentally challenges the legitimacy of the market as the basis of economic thought. Moreover, Doughnut Economics is a j'accuse to almost all mainstream political parties that blindly take economic theories for granted and base their entire policy platforms on the narrow scope of neoliberal factoids.

"For me, the commons is a way of broadening peoples' economic perspectives." Kate Raworth says, "And it's much needed too. Even just that new and smaller position of economics, as just a subsystem, is too radical for most mainstream economists."

In the 'Doughnut', the economy is divided into four fundamental ways people provision for their wants and needs. Raworth explains: "We all know the market and the state," she explains. "Those two have been the subject of an ongoing ideological boxing match, fighting over which side can deliver the most growth. And old economics has been so focused on them, that we have lost sight of the household, the space in which caring work is done and the commons. We've massively over-emphasized the market and the state. The commons and the household have been neglected for decades if not centuries. So we are not very skilled at those two systems anymore."

That's why I tell economists that if you ignore the commons, you're ignoring one of the most vibrant spaces of the 21st century economy.

While lambasting economists and policymakers, Raworth also offers an optimistic vision full of hopeful ideas and insights. "Elinor Ostrom was briliant in showing the commons in a fishing area or a piece of farmland. Add to that the incredible potential of the digital commons. I think both her Nobel Prize and the rise of the digital commons mean that the commons is going to become resurgent. That's why I tell economists that if you ignore the commons, you're ignoring one of the most vibrant spaces of the 21st century economy."

A new Politics of Belonging

Out of the Wreckage endeavours to lay the groundwork for a "new politics of belonging", as George Monbiot himself puts it. And just as in the Doughnut, the commons are at the heart of this new progressive narrative. "Kate talks about the commons as a starting point for her new vision on economics and I look at the commons for their potential for political renewal. We both agree that this is mostly a difference in nuance, our visions on the commons are very connected."

Monbiot carves out a path towards these new politics. "We need to build bridging communities within geographical neighbourhoods, we need a participatory economy, we need to implement democratic innovations and we need the commons. I see the commons as a re-democratising space." Prospering communities, he explains, are founded on thick networks that foster a culture of collaboration, in which "being an involved citizen" is no longer the exception, but the norm. That is when political change happens.

"Participatory democracy is crucial in reclaiming trust in our political systems. It allows us to re-gain a sense of ownership over our political systems." Monbiot describes the current representative system of democracy as "preposterous". "We vote for a government every four years and that government then assumes a mandate for everything it wants to do for the next four years, even for things that were not in their manifestos. It is an assumption of consent. No wonder we are alienated from politics, no wonder we don't trust our leaders anymore."

Participatory democracy is crucial in reclaiming trust in our political systems. It allows us to re-gain a sense of ownership over our political systems.

Monbiot says participatory budgeting is another essential step towards political renewal. In the Brazilian city of Porto Allegre, for instance, people of many different backgrounds re-claimed a role in policymaking by pioneering new ways of setting the municipal budget together. As Monbiot says, "if you can do it there, you can do it anywhere."

The final step is economic transformation. "Very much in line with Kate's vision, we need to start shifting resources out of the market and the state and into the commons. Let's start by moving land out of the hands of the private sector and into the hands of the community and the commons."

The Potential of the Digital Commons

The commons are the protagonist in the new story that Raworth and Monbiot are trying to tell. They offer an untapped potential in economic terms and they form the cornerstone of the new political discourse that is emerging from the wreckage of opaque representative democracy and free market fundamentalism. Their hopeful message is that we are only at the beginning.

That promise is exemplified in new technology, according to Raworth. "Twenty-first century technologies and the digital commons offer incredible potential. Look at how we generate energy, how we run machines, how we communicate and how we create and share knowledge. These forces were always centralized, by design. Energy came from an oil rig, production was done in a factory, communications came from an operator's switchboard and knowledge was held under patent and copyright.

"Now, thanks to distributive technologies like solar panels on your own roof or 3D printing, you can literally own your own production system. Communication has also been transformed into a distributive force, thanks to smartphones that allow each and everyone to become a node onto the network. Even knowledge is now being re-distributed, thanks to Creative Commons and commons-based licenses. All these developments completely flip the idea that you have to separate the workers and the means of production. The production means used to be so big that no one, apart from the upperclass, could own or manage their own. But now, they are so small, they fit in your pocket. This is revolutionary."

> The first internet was open source and non-commercial and slightly utopian. The second version of the Internet was captured. So let's see the possibility and make the internet 3.0 truly distributive.

Raworth continued: "We've only just begun to see how the commons work. But we already know that it is near zero-marginal cost to operate in the digital commons. So it offers huge opportunities. All we have to do is learn the skills needed to make something, to collaborate. That is the art of the commons. The potential is unprecedented. I feel a great excitement about what's going to happen."

Does that mean that technology will solve everything? "No, not at all," says Raworth. "There is a total bifurcation of how this can go. Right now it is not going in the right way. Networks have the potential to be distributive, but because of their architecture, they have just as big a potential to be captured. By itself, it is never going to go well. All this centralised infrastructure, these captured networks, that is really just 'Internet 2.0'. That's not the end of the Internet. We are just beginning. The first internet was open source and non-commercial and slightly utopian. The second version of the Internet was captured. So let's see the possibility and make the internet 3.0 truly distributive. There is nothing inherent about these networks that says they will be captured or distributive. We have to put in place regulation that make it distributive and keep it distributive."

The commons fallacy

Monbiot and Raworth also agree on their analysis of the misunderstandings about the commons. The commons are not tragic, as Garrett Hardin had famously asserted3. Or as Monbiot puts it: "Garrett Hardin, as it turns out, had never actually encountered a commons in real life before. He didn't even know how they worked in theory, let alone in practice. He didn't even know what a commons was. He mistook a commons for an open access regime. An open access regime is something entirely different. Oceanic fisheries are open access, for instance. Anyone can plunge in, drop a net and catch some fish. As a result, they are massively overfished."

Successful commons are tightly regulated systems. Hardin presumed that a commons has no regulation. In some ways, argues Monbiot, a commons is more effectively regulated than either a state or a market system. "Because you have the whole community involved in decisions, making sure that those decisions are equitable, that they are made by the collective mind, and that they reflect the needs of the whole community."

> Neoliberalism claims that the market is the only legitimate sphere and that when states seek to change social outcomes, they act illegitimately. That belief has been internalised by us all.

"We Are in Control"

Democracy and its flaws constitute another unifying element of the vision of these two thinkers. This is a topic that is ever more controversial in times of Brexit. But Monbiot is adamant. "The Brexit campaign was won using the slogan 'Take Back Control'. This was actually a really good slogan. There is an urgent need felt by many people in this country and in many other countries to take back control over their lives."

Monbiot says governments have become managerial and technocratic. "We have less and less purchase on the decision-making that affects our lives. We believe less and less in the government as a force for social change. We trust less those who govern us. Neoliberalism claims that the market is the only legitimate sphere and that when states seek to change social outcomes, they act illegitimately. That belief has been internalised by us all. It is very hard for us to shake. We have come to lose the idea that we can change our lives through voting in governments that are more *dirigiste*."

Democratising our systems means granting control over decision-making processes, treating people as intelligent citizens, according to Monbiot. "Evidence from all over the world shows that people respond like intelligent citizens when you treat them as such. We make informed choices because we recognise that power has been placed in our hands. This can lead to remarkable phenomena. At one point, in Porto Allegre, people took to the streets demanding their taxes were raised. It seems bizarre, but it makes perfect sense: if it takes you three hours everyday to get to work, you feel incentivised to improve the public transport system. The idea of re-engaging people in decision-making processes is one of the great strengths of the commons: we are in control."

> Mainstream economics only looks at people as highly individualized, ego-driven creatures. But there is so much more to us than just the homo economicus.

Monbiot concludes that democratising our systems is empowering. "It means giving back meaning, purpose and utility. This is about the fundamentals of human flourishing. Without meaning, purpose and utility, we fall into despair. Feeling useful to others, and as an active citizen, you feel useful to yourself and to the people around you. This is a fundamental human need, wanting to feel useful. People get depressed when they feel useless."

Re-Frame Ourselves to Re-Frame Reality

To fundamentally change the system, both authors argue, a paradigm shift is needed. For Raworth, that shift happens when we change the way we look at ourselves. "Look at human nature, look at all the different characteristics we carry within ourselves. Mainstream economics only looks at people as highly individualized, ego-driven creatures. But there is so much more to us than just the homo economicus. In the household we are partners or parents, neighbours or friends. In relation to the state we are voters, protesters, residents, service users. And in relation to the commons we are creators, repairers, makers and stewards. Economics tells us we are only labourer, consumer and producer. That is a very narrow depiction."

The way we frame reality, re-enforces that reality, Raworth explains. "There are traits they tell us we have. And when we are told over and over again about those traits, they are activated and stimulated. It becomes self-fulfilling. But there is a much richer story to be told, if you look at the other traits of human beings. That to me is the beginning of the paradigm shift. Start with a different picture, a much richer picture."

The Predistribution of Wealth

Raworth's Doughnut offers another major discursive shift that politicians and economists alike should take heed of. "These days, most progressive economists and politicians talk about redistribution and taxes. What they are really doing is just accepting that the system is the way it is, and that taxes are needed to even it out, from those that have a lot to those that do not have enough. They debate what the top tax rate should be, or what a minimum living wage should be. But we should go beyond redistributing income, to predistributing the sources of wealth creation. Do we agree that fundamentally, wealth lies within the potential of every human being? Then everyone should have a stake in the sources of wealth creation."

> Access to knowledge is access to means of wealth creation. We don't have to own the idea, we collectively add to the idea, we share it, we remix it, and by doing so, we collective create new ideas.

Predistributive measures are those that prevent the rise of economic inequalities before they occur, as opposed to state measures that try to mitigate them after the fact, through taxation and other similar actions. Examples of predistributive design of economic systems, Raworth claims, are abound. "We have just left behind us a century of corporate ownership. The worker used to get a wage and the capitalist would get his dividend. Thanks to the decentralisation of the means of production, we now see the potential for small-scale employee-owned enterprises. There, the return on the business stays with those who did the work."

Access to knowledge is another good example, Raworth says. "Access to knowledge is access to means of wealth creation. We don't have to own the idea, we collectively add to the idea, we share it, we remix it, and by doing so, we collectively create new ideas."

Shaping the Commons in Europe

Our conversation could not have been more timely with the European Elections around the corner. Both Raworth and Monbiot have clear ideas about what the EU could do to advance the commons. "I think the EU is uniquely placed to tackle environmental breakdown by transcending national interests", Monbiot says. "This is an existential crisis that nations have singularly failed to respond to effectively. This is not just about climate breakdown, which everybody thinks of first, but actually, there are natural breakdowns happening even faster than that. The loss of fertile soil, the loss of ecosystems cascading in ecological collapse in many parts of the world. Some of them accelerated by policies like the Common Agricultural Policy and the Commons Fishery Policy. The horrendous impact of biofuel, like biodiesel coming from palm oil."

> The EU needs to recognise the existence of the commons and make space for them. The commons is about networks. Networks need nodes to connect. The EU needs to conceptualize the commons, facilitate those nodes and be a partner state to the commons.

Raworth agrees. "At the European level, you have the possibility of scale. For instance, if a small town wants to build a circular economy, it will be hampered by the fact that they are tied into a national network of goods and services and regulations. The EU can change this, to empower local towns to be the change. The EU could ban all but three sorts of plastics and require them to be recycled. They could ban landfills. This would have such an impact, that it would create market opportunities. This offers opportunities of scale for entrepreneurs."

At best, Monbiot argues, the EU should be a truly transnational organisation. "That organisation should be able to manage the transnational commons. Right now the EU treats some parts of the commons like an open access regime, like the atmosphere. We need to turn that into a commons. And only institutions that transcend national interests can make that shift. Only the EU can start turning our open access dump into a commons in which we feel we all have a stake and we all a responsibility."

"I agree," Raworth says, "the EU needs to recognise the existence of the commons and make space for them. The commons is about networks. Networks need nodes to connect. The EU needs to conceptualize the commons, facilitate those nodes and, as Michel Bauwens would say4, be a partner state to the commons. I would add that something that the EU can do that private companies will never do, is to have a vision of a place we want to get to. This is why I like Mariana Mazzucato's work, talking about the role of the state to foster a vision5, to shape the direction we are going in."

Bringing Down the Old and Promoting the New

Both Raworth and Monbiot emphasize that we cannot merely depend on politicians and experts to bring forth the change that is needed. "Any sustained political change is going to have to be underpinned by social movements," says Monbiot. "They are the backbone of societal change. And they always will be."

"This transition we talk about is not easily going to come about," says Raworth. "The old is going to hang on for as long as it can to the power it has and to the narratives that it holds. A lot of energy will have to go into bringing down the old and promoting the new. Each of us have to decide what energizes us, where we choose to work. I personally like bringing up the new. There is nothing more powerful than showing a real example and saying: 'Yes, this is real, this is happening, it obviously works, so stop saying it will never work'.

"Some social movements are very much against the old, and we really need them too. Others are focusing on making the new thing happen, and we need those too. More than a hundred cities are now producing more than 70 percent of their energy from solar and hydro. Let's tell those stories of regenerative practices that are coming into play to say: this is happening.

"So, old power will absolutely resist this", says Raworth. "We'll see that the old and the new will ride along side each other for a while, in a very uncomfortable way. And there will be continued disruptions and challenges, like Brexit. Or new technologies. Or schools and students on climate strike. The question is, will we allow these disruptions to be captured by the old powers? Brexit is a perfect example of this. The Conservative and the Labour parties both have exceptionally positive hopes for their versions of Brexit, and those are both unrealistic. Will disruptions be captured by the old powers to extend themselves, or can we harness them for the new?"

3. COMMONS-BASED RENEWABLE ENERGY IN THE AGE OF CLIMATE COLLAPSE

David Hammerstein

Commons-Based Renewable Energy in the Age of Climate Collapse

by David Hammerstein

"… the main lesson to be learned from the collapses of past societies is that a society's steep decline may begin only a decade or two after the society reaches its peak numbers, wealth, and power."
-Jared Diamond, Collapse[1]

One of the fallacies in our unrealistic thinking about the future is the idea that renewable energy can substitute the fossil fuels that have been the basis of economic growth over the last two centuries. The "100% renewables" slogan suggests that all we have to do is change energy technologies in order to go on with business as usual. This techno-optimist marketing spin reinforces a certain social complacency, leading us to grossly underestimate the great challenges that a real energy transition would pose. The global collapse of our environment and our climate demands much more than a change in our energy production model. It requires us to question the basic premises of our extractive models of agriculture, industry, tourism, transport and construction.[2]

A simple 'tech-fix' approach to renewables is promoted to avoid structurally challenging the basic premises of our growth-dependent and extractive economies that cause most of the current life-threatening climate disorders and extinctions. We can only approach 100% renewables in a socially fair and environmentally sustainable world if we substantially reduce our use of energy and resources by shrinking our physical economies, especially among the wealthiest, most consumerist 20-30% of the global population. This de-growth of our economies is not possible only by means of technical efficiency measures. It requires major political change and state regulations in favor of sufficiency and the preservation and regeneration of the global natural commons. This is a daunting task.[3]

Today, solar energy and wind energy represent only around 2% of our global energy mix, while fossil fuels supply over 80% of our energy needs. A rapid substitution of fossil fuels by these renewable sources would demand a war-like mobilization of people and financial means that today is nowhere to be seen on the political horizon. Our energy transition has not even begun in earnest while our window of opportunity for slowing catastrophic climate change is rapidly closing. Today 98% of global trade, 100% of aviation, 99% of vehicles, 99% of construction, over 90% of agriculture and the vast majority of household heating are powered by fossil fuels. The increase of renewables, which is around 5% of current energy production (mainly hydroelectric power and biomass), is almost exclusively focused on electricity, even though electricity only represents 18% of global energy use. The other 82% is used mainly for heating, transport, industry and agriculture, among other activities. In total contradiction to what is now needed, global energy demand grew 2.1% in 2017 while CO_2 emissions rose 1.4% amidst growing and more desperate calls for drastic CO_2 reductions from the scientific community.[4,5]

To be realistic about our energy crunch, we must first exit the denial consensus. Due to ecological constraints, our present growth-driven and expansive economy based on cheap fossil fuels cannot be maintained. We are living the beginning of the end of a historical anomaly of sustained economic growth based on access to abundant, easily accessible fuels and other raw materials. But it is precisely this economic growth that has facilitated the growth of liberal democratic societies and the consolidation of individual freedoms and human rights. The structural lack of sustained global economic growth, coupled with climate change, resource scarcity and ethnic conflicts are stressing our democratic liberal societies. These situations are increasingly exploited by extreme right-wing authoritarian and populist movements.

> Major political, economic and cultural shifts towards sufficiency, self-contention, sharing, social equality and redistribution of wealth need to take place to avoid violent societal collapse.

Nevertheless, we can still try to mitigate or prevent this crisis. We need to consciously slow down and re-orient our economies toward re-localization of production and the regeneration of communities and nature. If we start now, the down-scaling of our economies can be done in a relatively organized and fair way, with relative social acceptance. Major political, economic and cultural shifts towards sufficiency, self-contention, sharing, social equality and redistribution of wealth need to take place to avoid violent societal collapse. If we maintain our present expansive course we might very well be condemned to an abrupt and chaotic economic stagnation that protects the privileges of the most powerful and locks out the majority of the population by means of violence and repression.

Most political leaders have placed all their money on one very improbable bet: the world economy will continue to grow indefinitely thanks to some miraculous technological inventions that have yet to be invented. This flies in the face of overwhelming scientific evidence of humanity's tremendous overshoot of the Earth's carrying capacity. Our leaders cannot act responsibly because they cannot escape their world view of never-ending global competition, extraction and economic growth that is impossible on a finite planet. They are ideological prisoners of a diabolical pact: in exchange for a few generations of intense economic growth with relative social well-being and democratic freedom, we shall all be forced to accept some form of autocracy in the context of environmental demise and scarcity.

The energy transition to confront climate change is not mainly about increasing renewable energy production but about quickly reducing CO_2 and other greenhouse gases: it is not principally about doing good things but drastically and urgently reducing the bad. More renewables does not necessarily mean less use of oil or gas nor less ecological destruction of our life support ecosystem. More electric cars does not mean less oil consumption by conventional cars, more organic food production does not mean less use of pesticides by intensive agriculture, more recycling and re-use does not mean less resource extraction. A "circular economy" that does not reduce the total volume of resource extraction can create an illusion of sustainability as explained by the "Jevons paradox".[6] To make a difference, renewables must substitute fossil fuels quickly and to the greatest degree possible, while overall energy and resource consumption must be reduced drastically. This is a monumental task that most politicians would say is totally unrealistic. But today's political realism has little to do with the needs of our future social-ecological well-being.

> More electric cars does not mean less oil consumption by conventional cars, more organic food production does not mean less use of pesticides by intensive agriculture, more recycling and re-use does not mean less resource extraction.

Any positive energy transition also needs to take into account in its cycle of life and value chain the preservation of biodiversity, fertile soil, rivers, forests, oceans and aquifers. The production and use of energy in industrial, agricultural and urban extractive activities contributes heavily to the destruction of our basic life support systems. It would be a horribly pyrrhic victory to finally achieve plentiful, cheap renewable energy while our systems of life-support of water, soil and biodiversity are fatally depleted and over-used in the very process of constructing an energy transition.

Relative decoupling of economic growth from CO_2 emissions is also a false path. Today there is no decoupling of economic growth from environmental destruction in absolute terms10 and even the relative disassociation of economic growth from the growth of CO_2 emissions is usually a statistical manipulation that does not count the emissions produced or accumulated in their imported materials, products and services from every corner of the Earth.[7]

The EU and the Tragedy of the Energy Anti-Commons

Climate change and many other ecological problems caused by the use of fossil fuels are an example of the tragedy of the commons, because the essential common resources of air, water, soil and biodiversity are under-regulated, over-used, over-extracted and over-exploited. These problems are also paradoxically an example of a tragedy of the anti-commons, because they are caused by unbridled and intensive enclosure, extraction and privatization of common resources. The influence of enormous energy companies on the EU and its member states through corporate regulatory capture, revolving-door corruption and strong lobbying strategies prevent stronger regulation of our climate-energy commons and protect the private rights of companies with dominant positions over key energy infrastructures and services. Today there are still legal barriers to the blooming and dominance of community-based or municipal renewable energy.

While large, centralized energy companies are starting to invest more and more in renewable sources, they are often not best suited for alleviating our social-ecological dilemma, primarily because they have little incentive to reduce overall energy consumption or to prioritize the social engagement of local communities in their commercial operations. The more energy they sell and the more energy is consumed, the more profits they make. The more centralized and rigid their physical and governance infrastructures are, the more vulnerable and less resilient they are to crises.

Climate technologies that can play an important role in energy transition are often not shared as quickly with countries in the Global South as they could be. This is partly due to intellectual property protections and a resistance to sharing know-how. In this conflict, the EU fights to enclose climate technology knowledge, which should be a common good, within United Nations forums (for example, the Paris Climate Talks in 2015), giving priority to European private industrial interests as opposed to calls from the Global South for more affordable access to climate-friendly technologies.

> There is a surprising over-confidence that the same centralized energy model that got us into this mess is also going to get us out of it.

In general, despite some recent positive legal change, the EU's energy strategy has been oriented primarily toward big energy companies promoting large gas pipelines, giant energy infrastructures, and modest CO2 reductions (still light years away from fulfilling global climate needs). Despite the fact that more and more Europeans are producing their energy locally or at home, most proposed European market regulations and budgets have not prioritized community-controlled or self-produced renewable energy, they have not offered sufficient financial support for community energy and they have not sufficiently defended the right to re-sell electricity among prosumers (at once producers of energy and consumers). EU policies have not sufficiently supported community-based feed-in tariffs or micro-grid infrastructures to support local renewables. Little has been done to eliminate massive direct or indirect subsidies to large gas, coal and nuclear projects.

There is a surprising over-confidence that the same centralized energy model that got us into this mess is also going to get us out of it. Instead it should be evident that without major social change in the relations of power between large energy companies and the common good, there will be no paradigm shifting energy change in favour of equality, democracy and a radical reduction of emissions. A much larger part of the EU energy budget should be earmarked for community renewable projects and compatible infrastructures, with broad citizen participation. This would help optimize resilient and more flexible energy supply costs through more efficient, short, and visible distribution loops while promoting flexible local energy autonomy. With this approach the EU would "commonify" a decentralised energy system as opposed to the current principal strategy of commodifying a centralised one.

The commons approach points at a number of problems and principles concerning renewables and the fight against climate change. In order to mitigate and adapt to climate disorder we need to focus on social and political strategies that prioritize solidarity, sufficiency and limits. The natural commons is both the source and the sink of our energy model. No one can claim ownership of the sun, the wind, the sea or the air. While it belongs to no one, we need to strongly and democratically regulate its use in a socially equitable matter with the aim of maintaining a sufficient level of sustenance of human and natural life.

> For a successful and rapid transition of our catastrophic energy model, we need strong political promotion of non-profit, decentralised, citizen-owned distributed energy systems that prioritise both consumer and climate profits over extractive private profits based on more consumption.

In the context of global climate collapse, much greater energy sobriety is a prerequisite of energy justice. Considering the finite carrying capacity of our climate commons, there is no sustainable way of alleviating energy poverty of people globally without at the same time alleviating energy obesity in wealthier countries of the North. When energy is governed as a common resource that is pooled by a community that governs semi-autonomous infrastructures, resilient sufficiency coupled with efficiency can take priority over expansion, growth and profits. Local stakeholders usually have very different interests from corporate shareholders. Large, centralised and privatized energy technology is often not appropriate for the real needs, the human scale of democratic control of a visible, circular and resilient local economy. In contrast, commons-based renewable energy is usually dimensioned to satisfy basic social needs that respect bioregional limits, boundaries and universal sharing.

Appropriate energy technology and knowledge developed with public money also needs to revert back into the regeneration of the energy commons by local communities (and with the Global South) through open source technology transfer or socially responsible licensing instead of being patented and privatised by private companies. Personal data on energy consumption and habits also need to be governed as a commons by local communities and municipalities without data commercialization or marketing by digital platforms.

For a successful and rapid transition of our catastrophic energy model, we need strong political promotion of non-profit, decentralised, citizen-owned distributed energy systems that prioritise both consumer and climate profits over extractive private profits based on more consumption. This means lower energy demand, greater social acceptance of new renewable installations and a new cultural paradigm that breaks with big centralized market lock-ins we have today, wherein most citizens cannot even imagine receiving energy other than from large multinational corporations.

This means turning public investments upside-down with a major shift toward localization. Instead of investing in giant centralised interconnecting power lines, the priority should be aiding the installation of community micro-grids where prosumers, producers and consumers are allowed to share, sell and buy community-based electricity production. This paradigm shift favours demand management, much greater citizen consciousness of saving energy and the building of flexible resilience. This must happen in the face of future social-ecological chaos and impending climate breakdown by investing in pooled district heating, renewable energy storage and increased local autonomy.[8]

We need the application of an EU energy subsidiarity principle on all levels of EU policy. This would mean that EU financing would be conditioned to support fluctuating renewable energy installations as close to the energy consumers as socio-economically possible. Large interconnecting power lines should only be built after implementing local and regional intelligent energy systems for fluctuating renewable energy. Majority citizen/municipal ownership of all new energy facilities should be supported by EU, national and local funding and legislation.

The EU's new "Clean Energy Package" approved in spring 2019 now recognizes citizen energy communities as an essential part of the energy transition. Now it is crucial that the rights of individual citizens or citizens collectives are actively supported institutionally on all government levels for producing, supplying and consuming renewable energy without any discriminatory treatment in favor of large private energy companies.[9]

The renewable energy commons is part of a larger strategy that at once regenerates communities and the living world through democratic governance, local control and common good values. The global multiplication of these energy commoning initiatives can play a key role in building the resilience, know-how and cooperation we desperately need to face the enormous social-ecological challenges of the coming years.

4. ENERGY COMMONS: THE MISSING LINK BETWEEN ENERGY TRANSITION AND CLIMATE JUSTICE

Cecile Blanchet

Commons-Based Renewable Energy in the Age of Climate Collapse

by Cecile Blanchet

In 2019, only oil lobbyists and shabby orange politicians persist in denying the influence of human activities on the Earth's climate. Scientific evidence is piling up and we know that we must change our ways. The concept of energy transition has become mainstream. However, governments have remained remarkably motionless. They are so inactive that kids strike school and demand climate justice in front of the United Nations' Conference of Parties. They are so immobile that citizen groups actually sue their governments for their lack of climate action. And when governments attempt to do something, it is so unjust that people take to the streets even during the coldest months of the year, screaming, filled with rage and frustration. Our leaders have forgotten that the poorer half of our societies should not have to clean up the mess produced by the richest half. That it should not be our kids cleaning up our mess.

Doing it Ourself

In the face of the lack of political will, an interesting and vivid grassroots movement has taken shape to reclaim our energy systems. From households to city politics, and even at the European level, there has been an unprecedented involvement from the public into energy and electricity matters. This has for instance taken the shape of energy cooperatives. According to the European Federation of renewable energy cooperatives, RESCOOP, there are at present some 1,250 energy communities in which a million people throughout Europe are involved.[1] Through the RESCOOP federation, these groups actively lobby at a European level to bend the legislation towards promoting and supporting energy cooperatives.

This model of energy cooperativism dates back to the late 1990s in Germany and was enabled by a set of disruptive laws supporting the production of renewable energy. This bill kick-started the German energy transition (dubbed "Energiewende"), which has become a landmark and is being widely copied.[2] The two main pillars were defined in the Feed-In Act of 2000: the priority of renewable sources to the grid and feed-in tariffs (fixed prices paid for renewable energy).

The particularity of this framework is that it has enabled small players to enter the game. Citizen cooperatives and households have especially benefited, because a fixed price for each kilowatt hour (KWH) could be sold back to the grid, which gave them more space to invest in new technologies. From the late 1990s onwards, the number of cooperatives in Germany has grown exponentially, reaching 900 in 2019.[3] It is a model that comes with many advantages. Let's virtually visit one of these cooperatives together.

The Revived Village

It's half raining and the landscape is dissolved in the mist when we enter Feldheim after a one-hour drive from Berlin. Apart from a large blue sign at the entrance of the village, nothing distinguishes the Energieautarker Ortsteil Feldheim (Self-Sustainable Village Feldheim) from the other villages in Brandenburg: all have similar houses with their neat little front-gardens along a similar straight road.

There's a bit of wind, it's cold and nobody ventures outside, except for our guide, Herr Kappert, his hat pulled all the way down, who comes to greet us. He leads us to the brand-new visitor's center. It's big and clean, and somehow reminds me of the over-dimensioned churches in small villages along the Camino de Santiago in France, designed to host the pilgrims on their journey. Indeed, I feel like a pilgrim reaching a Mecca for community-based off-grid energy projects. Once pointed in the right direction, we see the big giants peering through the fog, all turned in the same direction and rotating out of phase.

Contrary to its appearance, Feldheim is very special. Its uniqueness does not lie in the fact that there is about one wind turbine for every three people here (47 wind turbines for 148 inhabitants). That is actually quite common in Germany nowadays, especially in the former DDR. The special thing here is that the inhabitants are largely involved in the project.

At the turn of the century, Feldheim was just another post-communist village in Brandenburg: people were leaving, the school had closed down and unemployment was affecting more than 25% of the population. But in 1995, a joint venture between the villagers and a small local energy developer,EnergieQuelle GmbH, installed a first batch of four wind turbines. The success of that operation soon led to the installation of another 40 wind turbines, a biogas factory, a solar park, a giant battery and a parallel electricity and heating grid. This means that the village is now self-sufficient in its energy needs. There are several other spill-over effects from these energy developments in Feldheim.

As we strolled through the village to go to the windfarm, I approached Mr. Kappert and asked him whether the price of the real-estate in the village has suffered from the installation of so many wind turbines. He looked at me a little puzzled, laughed and said: "no, not at all, why?" So I explained that people in the media often talk about the opposition from local populations to windfarms and the recurring argument of plummeted prices of real-estate next to large projects. Mr. Kappert said that the project is an asset to the village and that it has probably increased the value of houses. And there is a major difference: external, imposed projects versus internal, self-managed and self-designed projects.

All over Europe, a movement to reclaim public services from the private sector is gaining traction.

In Feldheim, the project was developed in collaboration with the population over a period of more than 20 years and has been designed to fit the needs and specificities of the village. For instance, the fact that the local industry is mostly relying on agriculture rendered the installation of a biogas production unit (which enables the conversion of animals' manure and land-crop waste into natural gas) desirable and efficient. This shows how important it is to determine the appropriate technology for a community.

As we chatted, Mr. Kappert told me that the success of the project had a snowball effect on the life in the village. The income generated by the windfarm could be reinvested in other local ventures, such as a company designing arrays for solar parks. This, together with the maintenance of the windfarm and the biogas unit, created jobs so that the employment rate is now virtually 100% in Feldheim.

How can such a model be spilling over in neighboring villages? What happens with families who do not have the financial means to get involved in the project, in which a sum of 1500 euros was required to enter the cooperative? These important questions regarding inclusiveness and reproducibility are not fully answered by the cooperative model and we must turn our sight to re-municipalization of electricity utilities.

Municipal Utilities and the Energy Commons

According to a recent report from the Right to Energy Coalition[4], poorer households in many European countries face moderate to extreme levels of fuel poverty. This means that these families can hardly access energy to cook and heat their houses. The report also shows that households spend an increasing proportion of their income on energy expenditure (which can reach up to 33%). Although affecting most strongly southern and eastern European countries, this problem is also seen in cities like London, where the government has issued a plan to tackle fuel poverty.[5]

All over Europe, a movement to reclaim public services from the private sector is gaining traction.[6] Municipal utilities are seen as a tool to control tariffs, steward the energy transition and fight energy poverty. And indeed, cities have a crucial role to play as they are accountable to all citizens and are thus by definition more inclusive than cooperatives. The re-municipalisation movement is complex and involves a large range of interactions between local initiatives and governments, intrinsic motivations and level of achievement (i.e., from full purchase to public-private-partnerships).

An aspect of the energy transition which is often overlooked is the need to drastically reduce our consumption of energy (a decrease by 50% is planned in the German "Energiewende" plan).[7] The cheapest and cleanest energy is the one which is not produced and not used: all power plants, even those harvesting renewable sources of energy, have large impacts on the environment (e.g., by using rare earth elements for wind turbines).

> The cheapest and cleanest energy is the one which is not produced and not used: all power plants, even those harvesting renewable sources of energy, have large impacts on the environment.

Energy efficiency and conservation measures cannot be undertaken by for-profit energy providers, because they have an incentive to sell as much energy as possible. Municipal utilities, by effectively shifting energy from the commodities market to the commons, can help to manage the resource more efficiently and have a decisive role to play. An example for this is provided by the Sustainable Energy Utility in the US state of Delaware, which is a community-based institution aiming at designing and financing local energy projects.[8] The idea is to consider the energy consumption of a community globally, with the primary aim being to save it: when energy is needed, the SEU should implement an appropriate renewable technology, and incorporate heat and transport systems in the design.[9]

> The next step is therefore to combine the governance model of cooperatives with the inclusiveness of municipal utilities in order to implement a fully democratic and just energy transition.

Although municipal energy utilities have a great potential in achieving a just transition towards cleaner energy, the question of the governance is not always adequately tackled. In Hamburg for instance, a successful citizen campaign and referendum in 2013 compelled the city government to buy the energy (electricity, gas and heating) networks back from private operators. Two publicly-owned companies are now operating the grids, but citizens are still seen as clients and have no decisionmaking power. The next step is therefore to combine the governance model of cooperatives with the inclusiveness of municipal utilities in order to implement a fully democratic and just energy transition.

In many places of the world, privatisation of the energy market led to the appropriation of productive land by large multinationals (think of solar farms in the Sahara to feed the European grid), with very little or no spillover for the local economy.[10] This could be described as cases of enclosure of the commons and energy colonialism. Furthermore, the present "over-grazing" of our finite energy resources, which results from our "energy obesity", questions the inter-generational liability: our right to access energy should be limited by the legacy that we will leave to our kids. Relocating energy in the commons (by de-privatising or re-municipalising) would be a powerful way to address these questions, by linking production to consumption and re-engaging our liability as energy users. Finally, considering energy as a commons would allow to benefit from the creative power and experience of commoners to manage and share the resource.

5. TERRITORIES OF COMMONS IN EUROPE: NICHES OF A MUCH NEEDED TRANSITION

Jose Luis Vivero Pol

Territories of Commons in Europe: Niches of a Much Needed Transition

by Jose Luis Vivero Pol

We have to move to a Common Food Policy instead of a Common Agricultural Policy (CAP, the European policy framework that exists today). That idea is gaining traction in more and more circles, from the proposal by the International Panel of Experts on Sustainable Food Systems – IPES Food to the European Economic and Social Committee. Hundreds of alternative food movements are already supporting the idea.[1] A shift like this would solve the current policy incoherence between the different EU policies, such as trade, food, agriculture, environment, climate, health and social issues. Right now, these policies do not row in the same direction.

Another good reason for leaving the CAP behind and moving towards a Common Food Policy, would be the disproportionate power of big agriculture and transnational food corporations in the European policy arena. They exert their influence through revolving doors and lobbyists that literally draft and amend EU guidelines. This corporate policy capture purely aims to maximise stakeholder profits instead of public health, environmental protection or food security. It leads to huge monopolies in food retailing and agro-chemicals, patented seed research and supply, land grabbing in many parts of Eastern Europe and food safety circumventions (for example, glyophosate or neocotinoids). It is already common place in scientific circles to call the current way of producing and consuming food, the industrial food system, neither fair nor sustainable. Our industrialised food system is one of the main drivers of planetary destruction.

As global warming already poses a threat to human lives and agricultural production, what is needed for the sustainability transition is indeed more democracy, more rational and forward-looking management of food-producing resources and a different moral economy for the entire food system. Based on my international expertise as a food security specialist and my scholarship on food systems in transition, I believe that we need to value food differently. We need to re-conceptualise the entire food system so that it bolsters human health, nature stewardship, farmers' livelihood and landscape protection. We need a food system that works for the common good, not just for profit maximisation. To get there, it helps to look at the food system through the lens of the commons. This has the potential to cure the myopia that makes food and food-related elements (like seeds, water, land, knowlegde) exclusively a matter of market transaction. The industrial food system values and governs food as a mere commodity and that is wrong. The meanings of food are more diverse than that, as I have proposed recently. In the multi-dimensional framework to understand the value of food to humans, there are economic and non-economic dimensions.[2] Some can be valued in monetary terms, others cannot. What is the price of a human right to be traded in the market? As food is essential to everyone's survival, its market price could be priceless when someone is in desperate need. How can the cultural importance of any given food be priced when that valuation is rather personal and subjective?

> We need to re-conceptualise the entire food system so that it bolsters human health, nature stewardship, farmers' livelihood and landscape protection.

These critical reflections imply that not all food values can be reduced to supply and demand market rules, in which food prices do not properly represent the multiple meanings food has for different people. These meanings and social constructs simply cannot be reduced to food prices. Commodified food is the most reductionist approach to food, where those non-economic dimensions are superseded and obscured by the tradeable dimension (represented by quantity, quality, size, place of origin, homogeneity, durability and other features appreciated by the industrial food system).

Within this current framing, food cannot be enforced as a mandatory human right and traded as a commodity at the same time. As long as we see it as a commodity, it cannot be governed as a public good by a nation-state or as a commons by a community. Market rules prevail over other allocation mechanisms. However, if we consider food as a human right (which is currently not the case in any EU member state), a public good or a commons, then we should broaden the debate and look at grassroots movements in Europe for inspiration.[3] The rejection of the narrative of food-as-commodity and the adoption of food-as-commons or food-as-human-right can be found in many new initiatives that are popping up in cities as well as in a myriad of customary practices that have successfully resisted the commoditization wave.[4] Did you know for instance that 12 million hectares of land in Europe are still managed collectively as a commons?[5] They include croplands, pasturelands, estuaries, coastlines, forests, mountains and rural roads in all EU countries. Common lands have nearly all vanished in European countries that actively encourage private or state appropriation of communal lands, such as Belgium and Germany. Some of these countries do not even have a legal status for common land. In France, Spain, Italy or Sweden however, there are still millions of hectares of "territories of commons" that enable people to survive.[6] Well-known examples are the oyster beds in Arcachon Bay, to the Water Jury in Valencia, long-term rental contracts of agricultural lands owned by communities in Nonantola or the Everyman's Rights that enable any Swede to collect berries, fish or camp in anybody's landplot.

Another example is from Galicia, my home region in Spain: the proportion of commonland is one fifth of the total area, legally owned and managed by those who actually inhabit in parishes.

Earth The "territories of commons" are reservoirs of:

- climate-adapted practices based on agro-ecologybiodiversity and fundamental ecosystems services;

- governance systems, based on centuries of experience, with their own institutions and regulations;

- cultural heritage and collective knowledge, accumulated for centuries and adapted to local conditions;

- participatory and de-centralized democratic mechanisms.

The commons require a collective search for new shared governance systems that work in different contexts. They represent political alternatives to the representative democratic systems that we now have in Europe: systems that are detached from citizens, co-opted by corporations, focused on economic growth and the exploitation of common resources.[7] Therefore, it is not surprising that there is not a single mention of the commons, commons-based food systems or collective governance in the current CAP documents.

And yet, as a word of caution: the territorial commons and the food-producing commons are not governing arrangements that are devoid of inequality, exclusion or discrimination of certain community members.[8] The commons, understood as governing mechanisms crafted by human collectivities, are embedded in the communities that have instituted them and in the formal states where those communities live. Therefore, the commons mirror the inequalities and hierarchies already found in those groups and countries. As human institutions, the collective mechanisms devised to govern the commons are far from perfectly fair and flawless, although they are useful and resilient. Those mechanisms are complex combinations of formal and informal rules, customary norms and modern laws, being in many cases legally protected or at least tolerated by the state mechanisms where those commons are embedded.[9]

New initiatives like Community Supported Agriculture farms (CSA) or Food Buying Groups are popping up everywhere, adopting a logic that goes beyond the price tag of a strawberry. These initiatives enable organic farming to be a coproduction of eaters and farmers, shar ing risks, restoring common sense in the food system. Eat what is in season, do not use agro-chemicals that kill pollinators. These initiatives, however diverse the motivations of their members may be, share a rejection of the absolute commodification of food. They seek to re-create the lost bonds between producers and eaters, to re-embed food into the moral economy and local environment, and to make non-economic food dimensions more salient and relevant.

A commons approach to food systems recognizes the multiple values of food that cannot be reduced to its economic transactions. Food is not only essential for everybody's survival, it is also a human right and a cultural determinant. It has been a public good throughout history, from the Roman Empire to the CAP subsidies today. To reduce it to just something with a price tag, like a car, feels absurd and awkward. Purchasing power cannot exclusively determine your access to such an essential resource.

> They share a rejection of the absolute commodification of food. They seek to re-create the lost bonds between producers and eaters, to re-embed food into the moral economy and local environment.

If policy makers are ready to shift from an agricultural policy focus to a food-related policy focus, they should take into account new and old food-producing commons and partner with them.10 The "territories of commons", rural and urban, customary and contemporary, are innovative niches of transition full of tasty and healthy organic food, institutional novelties, digital technologies, participatory democracies and enviromental caring practices. Local solutions to the challenges affecting the industrial food system already exist. They are a complex set of self-regulated actions and state-imposed laws that succeed relatively well to satisfy community needs to govern common resources. Enabling food democracy, in which food citizens can re-gain control of their food systems, would indeed bring us closer to the values and the benefits of a regime based on the food commons. The aim would be sustainable agro-ecological production using open-source knowledge, seeds, fish stocks, land, forests and water as commons to reach food and nutrition security for all Europeans, as a commonwealth.

The change I propose is as much about technologies, subsidies, legal frameworks or specific policies as it is about moral shifts and narrative changes. This change implies devolving power to local communities to command their own transition pathways to reach fairer and more sustainable food systems. In walking that path, communities may fail or succeed, and other stakeholders such as the state and the market may or may not find a constructive role in that transition. But all of them shall value food and the food-producing resources differently than before. Considering food as a commons, a public good and a human right is an aspirational and inspirational narrative that may substantiate the proposed Common Food Policy, by unlocking political innovations that have not been explored so far. Let's dare to do it.

6. SOCIAL CIRCULARITY: FOOD-SHARING PLATFORMS ARE RE-INVENTING URBAN SOLIDARITY

Thomas de Groot

Social Circularity: Food-sharing Platforms Are Re-inventing Urban Solidarity

by Thomas de Groot

Foodtopia started three years ago in Murcia, a university town in the southeast of Spain. Initially just a pop-up kitchen on the university campus, it was run by a collective of four passionate people from various backgrounds, from engineering to retail. "We were, and still are, worried about the future that we leave to our grandchildren", says Jesús, one of the founders. "That is why we wanted to start a revolution in the perverse food industry".

And revolution is still needed, they claim. "The planet is warming at an alarming rate and as a global community we are simply not doing enough. People are already dying from climate collapse all over the world. The chaos will increase. Meanwhile, ignoring warnings from everywhere, we keep talking about economic growth. Our political representatives have abandoned us, or so it seems."

The idea behind Foodtopia was to ask people to bring their leftover food to this campus kitchen, in order to turn it into communal meals for all.[1] The response was overwhelming right from the start. Within a few weeks, the Foodtopia crew were feeding hundreds of people per day. Now, they have food hubs in many other towns and villages, that run complete circular systems, from local agriculture to production to communal meals.

"We are learning a lot from the urban farming revolution that happened in Cuba in the 1990s", Jesús explains. After the Soviet Union collapsed, Cuba lost their main trading partner. That, combined with stifling economic sanctions from the US, they had no choice but to radically change their agriculture and economy in order to stop the ensuing famine. Cubans turned to urban farming on a massive scale, pioneering techniques that people still use today, all over the world.

Food is more than just a means of sustenance, the people behind the Foodtopia project claim. It is the basis for community building, for civic life. Gathering food, or growing it, cooking together and organizing meals, it is all part of creating healthy and inclusive communities. And community members can only do their part to stop climate change if they work together. Jesús explains that Foodtopia strives for resilience in local food systems and that they all have a strong sense of urgency. "We have all seen the studies: our planet will collapse if we continue on this path of carbon dependence.

Degrowth is the only real solution."

The Spaniards are not alone in their conviction. In cities all over the world, organizations are creating new social practices by building communities around food. Some work exclusively with food waste, others don't. Some never charge any money for the meals and others expect one or two euros in return. But all share the belief that food stands for something much more: it is a symbol for civic sovereignty and social revival. "People need to feel sovereign in their neighbourhood", says Jesús. "Food turns out to be the perfect starting point for strengthening the community by sharing resources."

> Food is more than just a means of sustenance. It is the basis for community building, for civic life. Gathering food, or growing it, cooking together and organizing meals, it is all part of creating healthy and inclusive communities.

BuurtBuik is a Dutch non-profit that fights against foodwaste by collecting surplus food from supermarkets, catering companies and restaurants in order to cook free meals with that food for everyone in the neighbourhood. It is also a movement to promote inclusive sustainability or, as they call it, 'social circularity'. BuurtBuik works with companies like HelloFresh, social organisations like the Salvation Army and institutions like the municipality of Amsterdam to raise awareness about foodwaste, social exclusion, poverty, loneliness and health.[2]

The Netherlands is one of the richest countries on earth, yet many Dutch people have lived mostly the adverse effects of thirty years of exceedingly neoliberal and austere policies. Decades of center-left and center-right governments have led to a paradoxal situation. Dutch GDP grows 1 or 2 percent each year, yet around 200,000 Dutch children and 8 percent of households live below the poverty line.[3,4] In cities like Amsterdam, 1 in 6 people live below the poverty line, 27,000 of which are children.[5] 7 per cent of the population (more than one million people) feel severely lonely. In Amsterdam, that group accounts for one-sixth of the population.[7] Lonely people have a statistically higher chance of being poor and vice versa.[8] Both poverty and loneliness are very bad for your health. In fact, lonely people that live in poverty have a health-life expectancy (the number of 'healthy years') that is 15 years lower than the average young urban professional that might live in the same street as them.[9]

All over The Netherlands, teams of volunteers organize BuurtBuik-meals in community centers. The meals are cooked using only surplus food from supermarkets and restaurants in the neighbourhood. All meals are always free and accessible for everyone. This is the formula that has made BuurtBuik grow out to become one of the most vital and inspiring initiatives in the country. The volunteers at BuurtBuik have set out to battle food waste, which is a huge problem. In Amsterdam, for instance, businesses and consumers together throw away more than 100,000 kilograms of good food each year.[10] If food waste were a country, it would be in the top three biggest polluters in the world, right behind China and the United States.[11] The emissions that are released to sustain our global food production accounts for one tenth of all human-made greenhouse gas emissions.[12]

Just working on one of these challenges, whether it is poverty or food waste, would be a daunting task for any organisation. But groups like BuurtBuik in The Netherlands or FoodTopia in Spain explicitly choose a systemic approach. This means that they see all of these challenges as part of one problematic system. So they feel it is only natural that they tackle all of these problems at once. "Less state, more neighbourhood", says Jesús. "We look for shared identities of our neighbours, we strive for social, political and economic ownership of people, of citizens. Our food system should be the empowering catalyst for communities of people to become once again the drivers of their own future."

> If food waste were a country, it would be in the top three biggest polluters in the world, right behind China and the United States. The emissions that are released to sustain our global food production accounts for one tenth of all human-made greenhouse gas emissions.

BuurtBuik and FoodTopia make us change the way we look at the system. Food as a system is a financial crisis, a health care crisis, a natural crisis and a social crisis, they seem to say. The planet will not survive if we don't change the way we produce, distribute and consume food. "Our goals are to eliminate emissions and plastics from the food sector", Jesús says. But there is more. "We also want to democratize food, make it more healthy, reduce water usage, increase the resillience of cities, eliminate social exclusion, hunger and political tension and serve as an inspiration to others."

This seems ambitious, he agrees. "But the problem is all-encompassing and so we need equally broad solutions. Food as a whole is responsible for a large part of global energy consumption, emission of greenhouse gases, plastic pollution, deforestation, fresh water usage and waste production. For the planet, food as a system is a real problem. And the need for food in general is the cause of most conflicts and social tensions. The affect of food on our health is massive, a large part of our health problems are caused by food."

BuurtBuik anticipates a real shift in the way people think about 'green' issues. "For us to really counter climate change, we must do it together", says Suzanne, one of the coordinators of the organisation's Utrecht-branch. "That is why our meals are always free. We turn everyone, from the guests that eat with us to the entrepreneurs who donate food, into allies in the fight for a living planet." The Dutch organisation also tries to push this mentality shift. "We try to get people to be a part of our fight against food waste. This can be as simple as eating one of our meals. By talking about food waste we try to get people to think about what they consume and what they waste. What do they throw away and why?"

By starting small, you can make a big impact", says Suzanne. BuurtBuik works hyper-locally, in various neighbourhoods. All over cities like Amsterdam, Utrecht and Eindhoven, there are local BuurtBuik-teams. The young people that run these teams try to change the people's attitude towards food. They work with foods and vegetables that are not so pretty anymore, but still very much edible. However, "you cannot taste what the food used to look like", says Suzanne. "In the end, it's the taste that matters."

> We turn everyone, from the guests that eat with us to the entrepreneurs who donate food, into allies in the fight for a living planet.

Foodtopia works local too. It is what makes it work. Jesús says: "We build and design factories in the heart of big cities. The innovative design makes them adapt to local urban production." From there, they distribute the food to smaller neighbourhoods and villages. This system of hubs is geared towards increased resilience. It allows for different menus, depending on local traditions. "It also keeps our carbon footprint low", Jesús explains. "We process our own basic materials like grains, vegetables and oils. We work with re-usable containers that people use over and over and we don't waste food so there is very little waste."

BuurtBuik follows a similar strategy, Suzanne says. "We use cargo bicycles to move the food around, so we don't produce any additional emmissions. By using food that would otherwise have been thrown out, we avoid water and emmission loss and make sure those investments in food will not go to waste. We aim to cook healthy. So not only do we save food, we also make a healthy 3-course meal out of it that teaches our guests what healthy food can be. By working locally we are in close contact with our guests. Any overflow of food can be taken home, in containers they have brought from home. This was we try to not only keep food waste down, but waste in general."

In recent years, the people driving the organisation, mostly students and refugees, have really started to make an impact on the popular discourse in the country. Policymakers and private actors now aknowledge the value of inclusive sustainability. In 2019, the municipal government of Amsterdam is creating a new food strategy that emphasizes the need for this social component to the food system. And all over The Netherlands, start-up entrepreneurs are launching businesses that focus on community wealth.

The philosophy and practice of Foodtopia and BuurtBuik represent the transformation, democratisation and politicisation of culinary culture. These are necessary steps toward an urgent ecological and social transition out of the impending social and ecological collapse. Or as Jesús puts it: "The cultural importance of food is critical to understand the ongoing ecological and social crisis. The globalization of the agro-industrial system has a harmful impact on the health of societies and ecosystems. Unfortunately, most of western food culture ignores the destructive consequences of agro-industrial practices. Cultural practices and stories focused on food neglect the intrinsic relationship between hegemonic food culture and the dominant economic and energy regime. We are still an exception, in that we are transforming food culture within neighborhoods by leading the way towards a counter -hegemonic culinary culture that is economically viable, socially desirable, and ecologically sustainable."

7. OSTROM IN THE CITY: DESIGN PRINCIPLES AND PRACTICES FOR THE URBAN COMMONS

Sheila R. Foster & Christian Iaione

Ostrom in the City: Design Principles and Practices for the Urban Commons

by Sheila R. Foster & Christian Iaione

This text is an edited and shortened version of 'Ostrom in the City: Design Principles and Practices for the Urban Commons' by Sheila R. Foster and Christian Iaione, published in the Routledge Handbook of the Study of the Commons, edited by Blake Hudson, Jonathan Rosenboom and Dan Cole (Routledge 2019).[32]

Introduction

If cities are the places where most of the world's population will be living in the next century, as is predicted, it is not surprising that they have become sites of contestation over use and access to urban land, open space, infrastructure, and culture. The question posed by Saskia Sassen in a recent essay — who owns the city? — is arguably at the root of these contestations and of social movements that resist the enclosure of cities by economic elites.[1] One answer to the question of who owns the city is that we all do. In our work we argue that the city is a common good or a "commons" — a shared resource that belongs to all of its inhabitants, and to the public more generally.

We have been writing about the urban commons for the last decade, very much inspired by the work of Jane Jacobs and Elinor Ostrom. The idea of the urban commons captures the ecological view of the city that characterizes Jane Jacobs classic work, The Death and Life of Great American Cities.[2] It also builds on Elinor Ostrom's finding that common resources are capable of being collectively managed by users in ways that support their needs yet sustains the resource over the long run.[3]

Jacobs analyzed cities as complex, organic systems and observed the activity within them at the neighborhood and street level, much like an ecologist would study natural habitats and the species interacting within them. She emphasized the diversity of land use, of people and neighborhoods, and the interaction among them as important to maintaining the ecological balance of urban life in great cities like New York. Jacob's critique of the urban renewal slum clearance programs of the 1940s and 50s in the United States was focused not just on the destruction of physical neighborhoods, but also on the destruction of the "irreplaceable social capital" — the networks of residents who build and strengthen working relationships over time through trust and voluntary cooperation — necessary for "self governance" of urban neighborhoods.[4] As political scientist Douglas Rae has written, this social capital is the "civic fauna" of urbanism.[5]

> Jacobs analyzed cities as complex, organic systems and observed the activity within them at the neighborhood and street level, much like an ecologist would study natural habitats and the species interacting within them.

This social capital —the norms and networks of trust and voluntary cooperation — is also at the core of urban "commoning." The term commoning, popularized by historian Peter Linebaugh, captures the relationship between physical resources and the communities that live near them, to utilize and depend upon them for essential human needs.[6] In other words, much of what gives a particular urban resource its value, and normative valence, is the function of the human activity and social network in which the resource is situated. As such, disputes over the destruction or loss of community gardens, of open and green spaces, and of spaces for small scale commercial and artistic activity are really disputes about the right to access and use (or share) urban resources to provide goods necessary for human flourishing.[7]

The urban commons framework thus raises the question to which Elinor Ostrom's groundbreaking work provides an intriguing answer. Ostrom demonstrated that there are options for managing shared, common goods which are neither exclusively public nor private. She found examples all over the world of resource users cooperatively managing a range of natural resources — land, fisheries, and forests — using "rich mixtures of public and private instrumentalitie."[3] Ostrom identified the conditions and "design principles" which increase the likelihood of long-term, collective governance of shared resources. In many of these examples, users work with government agencies and public officials to design, enforce and monitor the rules for using and managing the resource.

> Is it possible to effectively manage shared urban resources without privatizing them or exercising monopolistic public regulatory control over them, especially given that regulators tend to be captured by economic elites?

Building in part on the insights of Vincent Ostrom, and others, she referred to this kind of decision making as "polycentric" to capture the idea that while the government remains an essential player in facilitating, supporting, and even supplying the necessary tools to govern shared resources, the government is not the monopoly decision maker.[8] Polycentric systems have multiple governing entities or authorities at different scales and each governing unit has a high degree of independence to make norms and rules within its own domain.[9] Polycentric systems also can unlock what she

NETWORKS OF TRUST & VOLUNTARY COOPERATION

POLYCENTRIC SYSTEMS

called "public entrepreneurship" — opening the public sector to innovation in providing, producing, and encouraging the co-production of essential goods and services at the local level. Public entrepreneurship often involves putting heterogenous processes together in complementary and effective ways.[10]

As such, our work has explored whether the commons can be a framework for addressing a host of internal and external resource challenges facing cities, and specifically to rethinking how city space and shared goods are used, who has access to them, and how their resources are allocated and distributed. Recognizing that there are many tangible and intangible urban resources on which differently situated individuals and communities depend to meet a variety of human needs, what might it look like to bring more polycentric tools to govern the city, or parts of the city, as a "commons?" Is it possible to effectively manage shared urban resources without privatizing them or exercising monopolistic public regulatory control over them, especially given that regulators tend to be captured by economic elites? Can the Ostrom design principles be applied to cities to rethink the governance of cities and the management of their resources? We think they cannot be simply adapted to the city context without significant modification.

Cities and many kinds of urban commons are different from natural resources and more traditional commons in important ways. This is why, starting ten years ago, we both began to explore the governance of the urban commons as a separate body of study. First, investigating individually how different kinds of urban assets such as community gardens, parks, neighborhoods and urban infrastructure such as urban roads could be reconceived as urban commons, and later jointly to conceive the whole city as a commons.[11,12] We realized that we needed a different approach to bridge urban studies and commons studies and therefore to pose a slightly different set of questions for the governance of the urban commons.[13] We also needed to define a different set of design principles for the management of urban commons in the city and the city itself as a commons.

> To say that the city is a commons is to suggest that the city is a shared resource — open to, shared with, and belonging to many types of people.

For this reason, we have been surveying and mapping 100+ cities around the world and 200+ examples of urban commons within them.[14] The goal of this research project is to enhance our collective knowledge about the various ways to govern urban commons, and the city itself as a commons, in different geographic, social and economic contexts. From this study, we have extracted a set of design principles that are distinctively different from those offered by Elinor Ostrom. They which can be applied to govern different kinds of urban commons, and cities as commons. Specifically, we investigate whether these design principles can help cities transition to fairer and more inclusive, sustainable, resilient futures given existing patterns of urbanization and the contested nature of urban resources such as public spaces, open or vacant land, abandoned and underutilized structures, and aging infrastructure. In our study, we see examples of how these resources can be governed as a commons in cities around the world.

The City as a Commons

To say that the city is a commons is to suggest that the city is a shared resource — open to, shared with, and belonging to many types of people. In this sense, the city shares some of the classic problems of a common pool resource — the difficulty of excluding people and the need to design effective rules, norms and institutions for resource stewardship and governance. Indeed, "the city analog to placing an additional cow on the commons is the decision to locate one's firm or household, along with the privately owned structure that contains it, in a particular position within an urban area."[15] Congestion and overconsumption of city space can quickly result in rivalrous conditions in which one person's use of space subtracts from the benefits of that space for others. For instance, different kinds of urban infrastructure (roads, telecommunications systems, water systems, parks) otherwise considered to be a nonrivalrous public good can become rivalrous either through increased demand or because of regulatory slippage.[16]

In addition to more traditional concerns about congestion and rivalry, the openness of cities also raises the question of distribution in the commons. Many contestations of city space and resources revolve around the question of how best to "share" the finite resources of the city among a variety of users and uses.[7] To be sure, distributive concerns fall outside of the considerations that motivated Garret Hardin's Tragedy of the Commons — i.e., consuming resources beyond the point where they benefit anyone and in fact reduce the overall benefit of the resource for everyone.[17] But Ostrom's institutional approach to managing shared resources applies to a much broader range of human behavior and social dilemmas than avoiding suboptimal results from the cumulative actions of rational actors.[18] Ostrom's work generated an approach that can be used in the analysis and design of effective institutions (or instruments) to manage not just common pool resources but many different types of shared resources.

The "commons," as defined by scholars who build on Ostrom's institutional analysis and development (IAD) approach, is as much a reference to community management or governance of shared resources as it is to the nature of the resource itself. "The basic characteristic that distinguishes commons from noncommons is institutionalized sharing of resources among members of a community".19 As such, it is not surprising to see the emergence of "new" commons — or nontraditional common pool resources — such as knowledge commons, cultural commons, infrastructure commons, neighborhood commons, among others.[20] These new commons seek to provide an alternative to the private/public (government) binary of governance solutions. These new kinds of commons focus on "communities working together in self-governing ways to protect resources from enclosure or to build newly open-shared resources".[20]

It is tempting, in asking whether shared urban resources (including the city itself) can be governed by local communities working together, to apply Ostrom's design principles to the city and to apply them to the management of many kinds of public and shared resources in the city. For many reasons, however, Ostrom's ideas cannot be wholly adapted to the city the way they have been used to understand the management and governance of natural resources. Ostrom's framework needs to be adapted to the reality of urban environments, which are already congested, heavily regulated and socially and economically complex. Without such adaptation, Ostrom's design principles will be lost in translation.

Ostrom's study focused mainly on close knit communities in which it was clear who was from the place and who was not (principle 1). For these communities, social control/monitoring and social sanctioning were two central pillars of Ostrom's design principles for the governance structure that communities often put in place to manage a common pool resource (principles 5 and 6). For this reason, she observed that rules of cooperation among users were written or modified by those who would be entrusted with both the duty to obey them and the responsibility to enforce them (principle 3). The fact that these rules were written by the same community of users that apply them suggested the need to leave some room for adaptation of such rules to local needs and conditions (principle 2). Of course, these structures and rules were premised on the assumption that communities' right to self-govern the resource would be recognized by outside authorities (principle 4).

> Ostrom's framework needs to be adapted to the reality of urban environments, which are already congested, heavily regulated and socially and economically complex. Without such adaptation, Ostrom's design principles will be lost in translation.

Ostrom found, however, that for more complex resources this governance responsibility or power was shared with other actors to form nested enterprises (principle 8). Notwithstanding the above, she observed that conflicts might arise because even the most united communities have internal fractions and therefore require accessible, low-cost tools to solve their own disputes (principle 7). These are the basic design principles which for years have been driving the study and observation of common, shared resources — namely scarce, congestible, renewable natural resources such as rivers, lakes, fisheries, and forests.

Cities and many kinds of urban resources are different from natural resources
and more traditional commons in ways that render necessary adjustments
to some of Ostrom's principles. First, cities are typically not exhaustible nor
nonrenewable, although they can become quite fragile over time due to
internal and external threats. There are, of course, natural resources such as
lakes, rivers, trees, and wetlands in urban environments that can be rendered
quite vulnerable by rapid urbanization, migration, and landscape change.[21]

Because they resemble in most ways traditional common pool resources,
researchers have approached the possibility for collective governance and
polycentric management of these "urban commons" in a similar fashion.[22]
However, much of the city consists of built urban infrastructure — open
squares, parks, buildings, land, streets, roads and highways — which can
be purposed and repurposed for different uses and users. In this way, these
resources —the kind of "urban commons" to which we refer — are quite
distinct in character and design from the forests, underwater basins and
irrigation systems that were the subject of Elinor Ostrom's study of common
pool resource governance.

Second, cities and many of their resources are what we might call
"constructed" commons, the result of emergent social processes and
institutional design.[23] As with knowledge commons, the urban commons
often require the creation of governance or management structures that allow
for not only the sharing of existing resources but also the production of new
resources which will be shared by a group or community of actors.[23] The
process of constructing a commons — what some refer to as "commoning"
— involves a collaborative process of bringing together a wide spectrum of
actors that work together to co-design and co-produce shared, common
goods and services at different scales.[24,25] They can be created at the scale
of the city, the district, the neighborhood, or the block level.

Third, cities do not exist in a pre-political space. Rather, cities are heavily
regulated environments and thus any attempt to bring the commons to the
city must confront the law and politics of the city.[11] Managing and creating
urban common resources most often requires changing or tweaking (or even
hacking, in a sense) the regulation of public and private property and working
through the administrative branches of local government to enable and/or
protect collaborative forms of resource management. Legal and property
experimentation is thus a core feature of constructing different kinds of urban
commons.[26]

Fourth, cities are incredibly complex and socially diverse systems which bring
together not only many different types of resources but also many types of

people.[27] Because of this diversity and the presence of often thick local (and sublocal) politics, social and economic tensions and conflicts occur at a much higher rate and pace than many natural environments. The economic and political complexity of cities also means that governance of urban commons cannot be just about communities governing themselves. Rather, collective governance of urban commons almost always involves some forms of nested governance — perhaps involving other levels of government and in most cases cooperation with other urban actors and sectors.[28]

Design Principles for the Urban Commons

Based on these differences, we began to think anew about design principles for the urban commons, taking into account what Ostrom learned about successful governance of natural resources commons. While many of her principles have clear applicability to constructed urban commons — such as recognition by higher authorities (principle 7), the importance of nestedness for complex resources (principles 8), the existence of collective governance arrangements (principle 3), and resource adaptation to local conditions (principle 2) — others are of limited utility or need to be adapted to the urban context.

For instance, communities should drive, manage, and own the process of governing shared urban resources, but we have seen time and time again that they can rarely avoid dealing with the state and the market. While this can be true of natural commons, and rural communities, we think both the state and the market are even more omnipresent in cities, making it difficult to side step them over the long run. As such, we observe that many types of urban commons tend to benefit from cooperation with other than internal community members and resource users. Rather, they need to collaborate and manage resources with other commons-minded actors, such as those constituting knowledge institutions and civil society organizations.

> Communities should drive, manage, and own the process of governing shared urban resources, but we have seen time and time again that they can rarely avoid dealing with the state and the market.

We have observed that in contexts where the State is the strongest, and markets are not as strong, local and provincial government actors can lend assistance to, and form a solid alliance with, communities to advance collective governance of urban resources. In this sense, the State generally acts as an enabler of cooperation and pooling of resources with other actors.

On the other hand, where the State is weak or weaker, either because of corruption or lack of resources, the market seems to be the only answer to enable the pooling of resources (i.e. human, economic, cognitive, etc.)

needed for collective action and collaborative management of urban resources. The market could subsidize the commons if proper legal structures and participatory processes are put in place and there is sufficient social and political capital among resource users to negotiate with market actors.

In both cases, the concept of "pooling" seems to capture the true essence of commons-based projects and policies in the urban environment. For these reasons, we have identified in our work two core principles underlying many kinds of urban commons as an enabling state and pooling economies.[11,29]

We also observed for instance that technology in cities plays a key role in enabling collaboration and sustainability, as well as pooling users of urban assets, shared infrastructure, and open data management. Further, urban commons-based governance solutions are cutting-edge prototypes and therefore often require careful research and implementation. In other words, they are experimental: new approaches and new methodologies are constantly being developed and require prototyping, monitoring and evaluation.

These basic empirical observations are now the cornerstone of a much larger and scientifically driven research project that we established and call the "Co-Cities Project." The idea of the "Co-City" is based on five basic design principles, or dimensions, extracted from our practice in the field and the cases that we identified as sharing similar approaches, values and methodologies.[30] While some of these design principles resonate with Ostrom's principles, they are each adapted to the context of the urban commons and the realities of constructing common resources in the city. We have distilled five key design principles for the urban commons:

• Principle 1: Collective Governance (or co-governance) refers to the presence of a multistakeholder governance scheme whereby the community emerges as an actor and partners (through sharing, collaboration, cooperation, and coordination) with four other possible categories of urban actors in a loosely coupled system;

• Principle 2: Enabling State expresses the role of the State (usually local public authorities) in facilitating the creation of urban commons and supporting collective governance arrangements for the management and sustainability of the urban commons;

• Principle 3: Social and Economic Pooling refers to the presence of autonomous institutions (e.g., civic, financial, social, economic, etc.) that are open, participatory, and managed or owned by local communities operating within non-mainstream economic systems (e.g. cooperative, social and solidarity, circular, cultural, or collaborative economies, etc.) that pool resources and stakeholders often resulting in the creation of new opportunities (e.g. jobs, skills, education, etc.) and services (e.g. housing, care, utilities, etc.) in underserved areas of the city or for vulnerable inhabitants;

• Principle 4: Experimentalism is the presence of an adaptive, place-based and iterative approach to design legal and policy innovations that enable the urban commons;

• Principle 5: Tech Justice highlights access, participation, co-management and/or co-ownership of technological and digital urban infrastructure and data as an enabling driver of cooperation and co-creation of urban commons.

These design principles articulate the types of conditions and factors that we observe are present and that instantiate the city as a cooperative space in which various forms of urban commons not only emerge but are sustainable. These conditions shape and define what we call a "co-city." The concept of the co-city imagines the city as an infrastructure on which participants can share resources, engage in collective decision-making and co-production of shared urban resources and services, supported by open data and technology, guided by principles of distributive justice. A co-city is based on polycentric governance of a variety of urban resources such as environmental, cultural, knowledge and digital goods that are co-managed through contractual or institutionalized public-community or public-private-community partnerships.

Polycentric urban governance involves resource pooling and cooperation between five possible categories of actors — social innovators or the unorganized public, public authorities, businesses, civil society organizations, and knowledge institutions —the so-called "quintuple helix governance" approach[31]. These co-governance arrangements have three main aims: fostering social innovation in urban welfare provision, spurring collaborative economies as a driver of local economic development, and promoting inclusive urban regeneration of blighted areas. Public authorities play an important enabling role in creating and sustaining the co-city.

The ultimate goal of a co-city, we believe, is the creation of a more just and democratic city, consistent with the Lefebvrian approach of the right to the city.[7]

Conclusion

The above design principles and practice are based on our observation and study of the ways that a variety of resources in cities, both existing and created, are being managed or governed by local communities in a cooperative fashion with other actors and often enabled by government bodies and officials. The five design principles, and some of the mechanisms through which they manifest, together with the co-city policy cycle/ process, compose the beta version of what we call "the co-city protocol."[30] We interpret such protocol as a language that could guide collaboration among urban communities experimenting with the governance of the urban commons, as well as the exchange of ideas and practices on the commons at the urban level without impairing institutional diversity and adaptiveness. Much like in the digital and open source world, this protocol would allow local communities to build a shared language that could be iteratively updated and could increase shared knowledge around the city, ultimately contributing to the construction of an urban methodological approach to the commons in the city and to governing the city itself as a commons.

8. DESIGNING, SUSTAINING AND DEFENDING RESILIENT URBAN COMMONS: THE STORY OF R-URBAN

Doina Petrescu & Constantin Petcou

Designing, Sustaining and Defending Resilient Urban Commons: The Story of R-Urban

by Doina Petrescu & Constantin Petcou

The question of the commons is at the heart of the discussion on democracy. According to Toni Negri, the contemporary revolutionary project that is democracy is concerned with capturing, diverting, appropriating and reclaiming the commons. The commons, in turn, have been created or are emerging as a key constituent process.[1] It is a re-appropriation, and at the same time a re-invention.

The question of the commons is also directly related to the discussions on the major environmental challenges we face: climate change, resources depletion and related economic and social crises. The environmental crisis is also a political crisis, a crisis of democracy and a lack of collective control over the resources of our planet, which is indeed our biggest commons. Learning how to govern our planet as a commons is part of the imperative of becoming more resilient.[2] Resilience is a term used to characterize the way in which systems and societies adapt to externally imposed change.[3] We understand resilience as a transformative condition, which allows us not only to adapt but also to transform and re-invent our society towards a more balanced, more equitable way of living on Earth. Elinor Ostrom convincingly demonstrated that the commons could constitute a resilient alternative to the current way of governing the world's resources.[4] She mainly studied traditional rural commons across different global contexts (exploring fisheries, forests, pastures) and has concluded on a number of principles on how commons can be successfully governed.

Urban Commons

Sheila Foster and Christian Iaione, two leading scholars in the emerging field of urban commons, have shown that the conditions are far more complex in cities.[5] Urban commons are 'constructed commons' that need a complex governance system. They involve not only commoners but also other urban actors who are external to the community of commoners. These actors are often in multiple interactions with a commons: public actors such as municipalities and the state, private actors such as companies and organizations - as well as various other communities.

Commons oblige architects to design collectively and accessibly, to take privilege and commodity out of design. In a long-term process of commoning, their design should assemble and mobilise, rather than segregate and exclude.

Urban commons have to be understood, designed, supported and re-invented as part of a complex process of transition towards more resilient forms of governance of the cities. For this we need new institutions, new protocols, a whole new infrastructure and agents to manage this process. When we founded 'atelier d'architecture autogérée', a collective of architects, we asked ourselves what we as architects can contribute to this. We realised that designing and sustaining urban commons is a special challenge for architects: it obliges them to design collectively and accessibly. It requires them to take privilege and commodity out of design. In a long-term process of commoning, their design should assemble and mobilise, rather than segregate and exclude.

R-Urban

This was the motivation for atelier d'architecture autogérée when we engaged with urban commons.[6] We started in 2001 with Ecobox, which was a community garden made out of recycled materials and a social-cultural center installed on a derelict site on Rue Pajol in Paris. We continued in 2006 with Passage 56 in the 20th arrondissement, which was a self-managed 'ecological interstice' instigating local ecological cycles in the neighborhood and enabling the production and recycling of most of its resources: electricity, water, compost and food. Although local, both of these self-managed projects generated local networks of urban commons, initiated by their stakeholders.

In 2008, we imagined a strategy model called R-Urban as an open-source framework that enables residents to play an active role in changing the city while at the same time changing their way of living in it.[7] The 'R' in R-Urban stands for 'resilience', a term that we understood in relation with the capacity of communities not only to take risks, but also to transform themselves in the face of rapid global economic and environmental changes. 'R' also signifies 'resourcefulnes', situating resilience in a positive light and relating it to the agency of community empowerment.[8]

Within the R-Uban framework we wanted to create a network of bottom-up resilience in order to give more agency to citizens and grassroots organizations around a series of self-managed collective hubs. These self-managed collective hubs host economic and cultural activities and everyday life practices that contribute to boosting the capacity of resilience within neighbourhoods. All of these hub also constitute a network of commons exploration, to develope and celebrate communities' resources: space, skills, knowledge, labour and creativity.

Designing

R-Urban has been conceived and initiated by architectural designers, yet the framework itself is co-produced and open to a wide range of actors. The first step in the implementation of the R-Urban strategy is the installation of physical infrastructure that would create assets for these new self-managed collective hubs. This can be achieved by using available land as well as other existing assets that could be used temporarily. In these spaces, change can be initiated, tested, learned and practiced.

The second stage would involve stakeholders who could use the space provided to share resources and training materials. Other allied organizations and initiatives would also be able to be plugged into the proposed network of civic hubs. The strategy would enable locally closed ecological circuits at the level of the neighbourhoods, balancing the activities of production and consumption: CO_2 emissions would be reduced, water and compost carefully managed and waste would be collected and transformed locally under the control of the people involved in the network.

In 2009, we succesfully pitched this model to the municipality of Colombes, a suburban city near Paris. We subsequently set up a partnership for a EU Life+ bid on environmental governance, with which we were successful. In 2011, we identified assets for three possible civic hubs: one for urban agriculture, one for recycling and eco-construction, and the third for cooperative housing.

Agrocité was the first hub, which we set up on a social housing estate. The plot belonged to the city and would be available for about 10 years. Based on this projected timeline, we imagined a demountable building, alongside a 1700 square meter plot of land that would included an experimental farm, a community-garden and a pedagogical garden. Another building included a small market, a café, a greenhouse and educational facilities.

The building and the site would function themselves under principles of economic and ecological circuits. The architecture and spatial organisation were meant to reveal and showcase these circuits, which otherwise would have remained invisible. These circuits would be part of a network that performs at a local scale, with the idea that it could progressively scale up to city and regional level. We started with the community garden as a way of engaging with the local community and the first harvest took place before we began to build. For the construction of the building we used re-cycled materials to showcase the ecological principles on which the strategy was based. From the beginning, we had an economic concern about the function of the building. Our aim was to host explicit economic activities (such as a market or café) at the same time as collective activities that have to do with informal social economies, such as exchange of skills and knowledge and bartering.[9]

We also prototyped a number of ecological devices. For example, we constructed a water-filtration device that was self-built with specialist help. It was the first of its kind in an urban setting. We also tested compost-heating, green walls, drip irrigation and a rainwater container to collect and use rainwater. We compiled quite sophisticated studies on watering and cultivation techniques for the poor urban soil we inherited. Urban agriculture in densely built suburban estates is a completely new field of practice, which explains why many of these techniques and devices needed to be invented.

Recyclab was the second hub we implemented, this time as a social enterprise. It is a recycling and eco-construction unit comprised of several facilities for storing and reusing locally salvaged materials, by transforming them into eco-construction elements. We set up a 'fablab' for residents to use. Both hubs were built with 'reversable design' on temporarily available public land. They could easily be relocated and rebuilt at any time. The reversibility is an ecological principle implying that the site can be repurposed by other urban programmes, according to evolving needs and conditions. The building itself can be dismantled and repurposed in a different context for different users.   .

The third hub, Ecohab, was planned to be a cooperative housing hub. Unfortunately, the project was blocked by municipal politicians.

Sustaining

Commoning involves making and sharing that which supports a community. The practice of commoning is at the same time the practice of becoming community: working out how to access, use, care for, take responsibility for and distribute its benefits. Commoning can take place on private or public property. It can be practiced around open-access resources, such as the atmosphere or waterways, over which there are no formal rules of ownership. It is very important to remember that all those involved in the R-Urban hubs are inhabitants of a working-class neighbourhood. Many are unemployed, and some are retired, but they have become the main stakeholders in these projects based on their self-employment or voluntary work.

> The practice of commoning is at the same time the practice of becoming community: working out how to access, use, care for, take responsibility for and distribute its benefits.

In the Agrocité hub there was a local market where produce from the garden, objects from Recyclab and local handicrafts were sold. Local economy and entrepreneurship were actively supported. A good example is one of the inhabitants who we supported to set up a worm compost business. We set up a compost farm with him and he produced compost for the garden in exchange for using the land for his wormery. He also set up a Compost School and received accreditation as a compost specialist trainer. He now makes a living as a trainer. Many local municipalities need such a specialist, since organic waste is now processed by public services. In two years, he has trained 160 compost masters and many of his pupils have now set up their own compost businesses.

R-Urban advocates a specific cultural and political change, which is to change how we do things in order to change our future. Our hope is that new collective practices of civic resilience can emerge, which both reduce the ecological footprint and contribute to reinventing relationships between individuals and collectives.

Such transformational change must take place at the micro-scale of each individual to enable the building of a culture of co-produced resilience at the macro-scale. Commoning means not only having the capacity to acquire space and managing it, but also having the capacity to build relationships that can be maintained and strenghtened into the future. The work of R-Urban has produced ecological repair in a region where much of the land was destitute. Non-human actors contributed to this work – plants, birds, insects, worms, bacteria – that somehow became part of the commoning community. 'More-than-human communities' emerged around the R-Urban eco-commons.[10]

Collective governance, as Elinor Ostrom demonstrated, is an essential issue for a commoning community.[11] Agreements are needed and a shared concerns must be expressed, not to destroy but to support community resources. In our case this was initiated through a series of gatherings and talks. Some were about decision-making, others were on very technical subjects, concerning how ecological loops could work. It was also important to bring external people to these sites, such as other organisations, institutions and researchers. This meant opening up the co-production process to those that were not the immediate users. As well as the crucial participation of the neighbourhood, the R-Urban governance strategy involved many local, regional and international actors. The project enabled a trans-local anchoring with the aim of greater sustainability.

Defending

Some institutional partners where more critical than others. One of the key institutional partners was the municipality, which was effectively the landowner. After the local elections in 2014, all those municipal agents involved in the foundation of the project left. They were replaced by a new right-wing municipal team with a very ambitious mayor. She was ideologically against the project and she decided that the municipality would stop the partnership and reclaim the space occupied by the R-Urban hubs for new private developments. This demonstrated how much the process of commoning depends on politics. We were missing a Partner-State.[12] It turned out that that was critical for the transition towards commons-based urban governance, to facilitate citizen initiatives and to guarantee sustainability beyond the whims of political cycles.

The local decision to dismantle R-Urban triggered a wave of solidarity amongst researchers and residents of Colombes. They have since engaged in different forms of protest against the new political reality. This was a new stage within the commoning process, which was now framed as an advocacy campaign and political struggle to defend the socio-ecological commons, to challenge the local government and claim recognition of the success of the project. A protest petition claiming the positive impact of Agrocité and the other urban units has collected 17,000 signatures. Finally, we lost the case in court for the simple reason that current laws protect private property and do not value the interests of common use or the social and ecological benefits of a civic project. We realised that continuing the opposition on site in Colombes would have only drained the energy of the community. We chose to give up on resistance politics and embrace the adversity by turning it into a new positive start. We decided to relocate the project to the neighbouring city of Gennevilliers, at a small distance from the former location, to be able to allow the users to continue with the project.

> A partner-state is critical for the transition towards commons-based urban governance, to facilitate citizen initiatives and to guarantee sustainability beyond the whims of political cycles.

In 2017, Agrocité was reconstructed in Gennevilliers and Recyclab was dismantled and rebuilt in Nanterre. Other municipalities have also shown interest and we have commenced R-Urban Bagneux, where we are currently building two new units. There is also a R-Urban unit in London. Instead of weakening us, our loss in Colombes emboldened us. R-Urban will grow. In order to strengthen the R-Urban commons, we have thickened institutional support and diversified our alliances. There is now a charter, a development agency and a regional network. The R-Urban network now has seven hubs with more than 500 citizens actively involved in using and managing the hubs. We hope that R-Urban will further grow into a civic movement for resilient urban commons.[13]

9. COULD THIS LOCAL EXPERIMENT BE THE START OF A NATIONAL TRANSFORMATION?

George Monbiot

Could This Local Experiment Be The Start Of A National Transformation?

by George Monbiot

One London borough has been bringing people together to work, socialise and dream. The results are extraordinary.

If there is hope, it lies here, in the most deprived borough in London. Barking and Dagenham has shocking levels of unemployment, homelessness, teenage pregnancy, domestic violence and early death. Until 2010, it was the main stronghold of the British National party.[1] Its population turns over at astonishing speed: every year, about 8% of residents move out. But over the past year it has started to become known for something else: as a global leader in taking back control.

Since the second world war, councils and national governments have sought to change people's lives from the top down. Their efforts, during the first 30 years of this period at least, were highly effective, creating public services, public housing and a social safety net that radically improved people's lives.

But they had the unintended consequence of reducing our sense of agency, our social skills and mutual aid. Now, in the age of austerity, state support has been withdrawn, leaving many people with the worst of both worlds: neither the top-down protection of government nor the bottom-up resilience of the community it replaced. I believe we still need strong state support and well-financed public services. But this is not enough. The best antidote to the rising tide of demagoguery and reaction is a politics of belonging based on strong and confident local communities.[2]

Those who study community life talk about two kinds of social network: bonding and bridging.[3] Bonding networks are those created within homogeneous groups. While they can overcome social isolation, they can also foster suspicion and prejudice, while limiting opportunities for change. Bridging networks bring people from different groups together. Research suggests that they can reduce crime and unemployment and, by enhancing community voices, improve the quality of government.[4,5,6]

After routing the BNP, which had taken 12 of 51 seats in 2006, Labour councillors in Barking and Dagenham saw that it wasn't enough to target people's needs and deliver isolated services.[7,8] They wanted to move from paternalism to participation. But how?

Just as the council began looking for ideas, the Participatory City Foundation led by the inspiring Tessy Britton, approached it with a plan for an entirely different system, developed after nine years of research into how bridging networks form.[9,10] Nothing like it had been attempted by a borough before. The council realised it was taking a risk. But it helped to fund a £7m, five-year experiment, called Every One, Every Day.[11,12]

> The best antidote to the rising tide of demagoguery and reaction is a politics of belonging based on strong and confident local communities.

Researching successful community projects across the world, the foundation discovered a set of common principles.[13] Typically, they demand little time or commitment from local people, and no financial cost. They are close to people's homes, open to everyone, and designed to attract talent rather than to meet particular needs. They set up physical and visible infrastructure. And rather than emphasising novelty – the downfall of many well-intentioned schemes – they foster simple projects that immediately improve people's lives. The foundation realised that a large part of the budget would need to be devoted to evaluation, to allow the plan to adapt almost instantly to residents' enthusiasm.

They launched Every One, Every Day in November 2017, opening two shops (the first of five) on high streets in Barking and Dagenham. The shops don't sell anything but are places where people meet, discuss ideas and launch projects. The scheme has also started opening "maker spaces", equipped with laser cutters and other tools, sewing machines and working kitchens. These kinds of spaces are usually occupied by middle-class men but, so far, 90% of the participants here are women. The reason for the difference is simple: almost immediately, some of the residents drew a line on the floor, turning part of the space into an informal creche, where women take turns looking after the children. In doing so, they overcame one of the biggest barriers to new businesses and projects: affordable childcare.

I visited the old printers' warehouse in Thames Road, Barking, that the scheme is turning into a gigantic new workshop where people can start collaborative businesses in areas as diverse as food, clothing and renewable energy. Already, the experiment has catalysed a remarkable number of projects set up spontaneously by residents.

There are welcoming committees for new arrivals to the street, community potluck meals, cooking sessions and street lunches. There's a programme to turn boring patches of grass into community gardens, play corners and outdoor learning centres. There's a bee school and a chicken school (teaching urban animal husbandry), sewing and knitting sessions, places for freelance workers to meet and collaborate, computing and coding workshops, storytelling for children, singing sessions and a games cafe. A local football coach has started training people in the streets. There's a film studio and a DIY film festival too, tuition for spoken-word poets and a scheme for shutting streets to traffic so children can play after school. Local people have leapt on the opportunities the new system has created.

> Talking to residents involved in these projects, I kept hearing the same theme: "I hated this place and wanted to move out. But now I want to stay.

Talking to residents involved in these projects, I kept hearing the same theme: "I hated this place and wanted to move out. But now I want to stay". A woman in Barking told me that "getting out and socialising is very hard when you're unemployed", but the local shop has "massively improved my social life". Now her grandad and mum, who were also isolated, come in as well. Another explained that, before the community shop opened in Dagenham, all her friends were in other boroughs and she felt afraid of local people, especially "the young hoodies". Now she has local friends with origins all over the world: "I no longer feel intimidated by the young guys round here, because I know them … It's been the best year of my adult life." Another, a black woman who had lived in fear of the BNP's resurgence, told me: "This is hope at last. Hope for my generation. Hope for my grandchildren."

There's a long way to go. Four thousand of the borough's 200,000 people have participated so far. But the rate of growth suggests it is likely to be transformative. The council told me the programme had the potential to reduce demand for social services as people's mental and physical health improves. Partly as a result, other boroughs and other cities are taking an interest in this remarkable experiment. Perhaps it's not the whole answer to our many troubles. But it looks to me like a bright light in a darkening world.

This article was originally published by George Monbiot on the website of The Guardian on January 24th of 2019 (https://www.theguardian.com/ commentisfree/2019/jan/24/neighbourhood-project-barking-dagenham)[14]

10. A NEW VISION FOR A SHARED DIGITAL EUROPE

Sophie Bloemen, Alek Tarkowski and
Paul Keller

A New Vision for a Shared Digital Europe

by Sophie Bloemen, Alek Tarkowski and Paul Keller

Digitalisation has led much of our interaction, communication and economic activity to take place in the digital space through data or over online intermediaries. What kind of space should this digital sphere be?

For the last 10 years, Europe has focused on regulating the digital space towards building a Digital Single Market in Europe. This approach does not suffice to address challenges that are ahead of us. We believe that seeing this space as a market place only does not do it justice. This space is in effect our society – a society that is experiencing a digital transformation. Therefore we cannot accept the digital sphere as a place where only market dynamics rule. Society is more than an interaction between market players and people are more than entrepreneurs or consumers.

Today, market orthodoxy limits our ability to deal with the domination by corporate monopolies that constrain both individual freedom online and the emergence of a truly European civic space. This market focus needs to be replaced with an approach that is society-centric at its heart.

We believe that Europe needs to establish its own rules for the digital space, which embody our values: strong public institutions, democratic governance, sovereignty of communities and people, diversity of European cultures, equality and justice. A space that is common to all of us, but at the same time diverse and decentralised. This requires Europe to enable self-determination, to cultivate the commons, to decentralise infrastructure and to empower public institutions.

Enable self-determination

Self-determination in the digital environment refers to the right to privacy and the need for more democratic models of data governance and algorithmic transparency. The call for self-determination in the digital environment is a reaction to the growing market power of a handful of platform providers who increasingly control the digital space. It is also a call for using digital tools to support sovereignty at community, municipal and regional levels. Technology should serve the common good and support broad citizen participation, instead of solely aiming for purely commercial objectives and outcomes.

Our daily lives are impacted by a globalised market in which such commercial entities are exceptionally wealthy and powerful. We not only use their products and services, but, especially within the digital space, share data about ourselves in exchange for free or discounted use of these products and services. Data-driven corporations extract value from users to process, trade and commercialise for maximum profit. Within this process, data is used to manipulate users and to further increase the consumption of products.

> Data-driven corporations extract value from users to process, trade and commercialise for maximum profit. Within this process, data is used to manipulate users and to further increase the consumption of products.

At the level of individuals, this translates into challenges with regard to users' personal data and privacy. At the level of the society, this becomes an issue of a market capture of data as a resource that is shaping our education, our housing, our transport, our environments, as well as our identities, according to commercial interests without any democratic debate on the direction taken. Citizens have no agency in this process and lack control.

This lack of control over data is not just an in issue with regard to commercial products and services. The public sector is increasingly relying on data analysis and algorithmic decision-making. There is a growing body of examples of detrimental effects from this type of automated decision-making on people in marginalised positions - and algorithmic bias can ultimately adversely affect all citizens.

By calling for self-determination in the digital environment we ask for something more fundamental than the individual legal right to privacy. It must be possible to fully participate in (online) social life without having to give up your (personal) data to commercial entities. The role of data and how it is used in surveilling and influencing users needs to be made transparent to the general public and users need to have meaningful opportunities to minimise data collection and control its use.

Yet, self-determination cannot be achieved by only thinking about protecting privacy in terms of individual rights. We need to rethink privacy as a public good, because the increasing use of personal data by tech companies and governments is not only impacting the individual, but has larger societal consequences. More broadly speaking, there is need for democratization of data governance aimed at improving our standards with respect to personal data extraction and processing. We need more robust oversight of these practices.

> The role of data and how it is used in surveilling and influencing users needs to be made transparent to the general public and users need to have meaningful opportunities to minimise data collection and control its use.

In this context we also see self-determination relating to solidarity. Solidarity in terms of not leaving everything to the individual but facing these challenges of the digital transformation as a collective. Collectively and in solidarity with each other we can set standards for a society that is democratic and where citizens are protected from commodification, privacy intrusion and surveillance. We should collectively work to realise a digital environment that instead facilitates self realisation, creativity and diversity.

Cultivate the Commons

The digital age has opened the door to many collaborative forms of creating, remixing and sharing knowledge and culture. The success of free and open-source software, tens of thousands contributors to Wikipedia and the flourishing open-design and manufacturing community are notable realms in which collaborative activity has transformed 20th century models of knowledge production. Hackerspaces and fab labs are massively pioneering new forms of distributed local production while tapping into a global knowledge ecosystem.

Creative Commons licenses use intellectual property law to place knowledge and culture in the commons. Developments in open science and innovation are changing the way science is being performed. Open science makes scientific research, data and publications accessible to all levels of inquiry: society, amateur, or professional. A key vehicle for disseminating scientific knowledge and maintaining it as a commons is open access publishing. The platform cooperativism movement, which sees digital platforms themselves as forms of the commons, is another example.

The digital-networked environment allows us to put a bigger emphasis on supporting commons-based alternatives to the market that have the potential to create huge social value. Developing digital spaces that are managed as a commons with appropriate governance structures is essential to creating a digital environment that is democratic and supports values at the heart of European societies. Spaces, resources and projects managed as a commons need to be seen as equal alternatives to market mechanisms.

Yet today, the digital commons are pushed to the margins of the online environment by commercial monopolies that over the years have overtaken the open sharing and peer-to-peer communication channels of the Internet. For each success of the digital commons - such as Wikipedia, which remains one of the most popular non-commercial, online platforms in Europe - we observe even more places where market logic limits the potential of the commons. The potential of digital technologies to offer open access to crucial knowledge and cultural resources is not being fulfilled. Similarly, spaces in which digital technologies are employed to share resources are quickly captured by dominant market platforms thant seek a commercial rent on the basis of the contributions of users.

> The digital commons are pushed to the margins of the online environment by commercial monopolies that over the years have overtaken the open sharing and peer-to-peer communication channels of the Internet.

The commons approach overlaps with or feeds into an emerging political discourse where wellbeing and social wealth are not defined in terms of narrow economic criteria like GDP or corporate profit. Instead it looks to a richer, more qualitative set of criteria that cannot be easily measured: moral legitimacy, participation, equity, resilience, social cohesion and social justice. It promotes a regenerative economy based on circular principles and its primary aims are to maintain a sustainable system for people and the planet. Local community and participatory culture are core building blocks of such a system.

Europe has the opportunity to strengthen, promote and facilitate commoning activities and commons-based production. European policymakers need to adopt a hybrid approach, in which market-based and commons-based solutions are considered side-by-side as governance models for core aspects, spaces and layers of the Internet stack. We need to identify situations in which a "commons-first" approach should be adopted. European policies that support open science and open access to scholarship and data in the European Research Area are a great example of such an approach. Supporting a decentralised, community-based sharing economy that supports local commons is something that can be legislated at the EU level and which will have a real impact on the ground.

Decentralise Infrastructure

Decentralisation is the basic shift caused in the past by core network technologies, from the original packet-switching networks, through peer-to-peer content networks, to currently developed blockchain-based solutions. Decentralised infrastructure is open, distributed and shared. It is an infrastructure that can also function as a commons, and can be governed in a democratic and self-determined manner.

In the last decade, centralised and even monopolistic services have been built on top of the decentralised infrastructure of the Internet. Since these are all very large and often non-European commercial entities, the centralisation of control over the digital networks is a form of market capture of a resource that should be treated as a universal basic service that needs to be governed as a commons. Centralisation of the Internet and the creation of online monopolies has been fueled by a successful shift to business strategies that focus on monetisation of data instead of content. This development has led to a concentration of power in the hands of a few dominant platforms, most of which are located outside of Europe either in the US or China. As a result, much of the development of the Internet and related areas of information technology is being shaped outside of the EU.

> The centralisation of control over the digital networks is a form of market capture of a resource that should be treated as a universal basic service that needs to be governed as a commons.

As the Internet becomes more and more ubiquitous, with Internet-of-Things solutions diffusing in the real world, the issue of (de)centralisation concerns more than just online data and content flows. The urban environment is intertwined with the way we manage knowledge and our web-based economies. Similarly, the current wave of technological change and disruption related to the broad class of artificial intelligence technologies has the potential to exacerbate centralisation.

In the last few years, Europe has attempted to counter the dominance of big technology companies by leveraging antitrust regulatory policies, which can be seen as targeting centralisation of the Internet within the boundaries of market-focused policies. Yet, decentralisation policy cannot function solely on the basis of regulation aimed at managing market competition - although it is a step in the right direction. Decentralisation is also a necessity because it can contribute to increasing democratic control. At the same time decentralization will not be the answer to all challenges, and should be regarded as being a rule that allows exceptions where it makes sense.

A decentralised approach to digital infrastructures should be applied at different levels of the technological stack of the Internet: First, decentralisation should remain a basic principle of the Internet. Second, decentralisation should be applied to the level of online services and should be seen as an alternative to the current model, in which data and content flows, communication and social interactions is captured by monopolistic aggregators.

An effort to decentralise the digital infrastructure must provide more room for public institutions and abstain from traditional approaches to solving societal challenges built on top-down control. We see public institutions as important drivers of a decentralised network of actors, who cooperate on 'missions' to face societal challenges at grand scale. Decentralisation of digital infrastructures that increasingly govern our societies could be such a mission.

Decentralising our technological infrastructure must aim at increasing

Europe's technological sovereignty by reducing dependency on non-European technology providers and to enable fair competition and ensure accountability of service providers. It must also take into account democratic traditions and historic diversity. As such it should provide more agency to European cities - cooperating in the municipalist movement - that are looking for ways to develop decentralised solutions that gain from the relative power and independence of cities as actors.

Empower Public Institutions

Europe has a long and rich history of delivering public goods and services through public institutions. Publicly-funded cultural heritage institutions contribute to our identity, and encourage learning and creativity. Public libraries serve as knowledge hubs and play an important role in providing access to marginalised groups. Public schools and universities are the bedrock of our educational systems and public service broadcasting organisations ensure the provision of quality news and information and allow for diversity of cultural expression. Public institutions are also best placed to assure broad democratic civic participation on how our knowledge, science and culture are governed.

The digital revolution has created the preconditions that would allow these institutions to better fulfill their missions by actively involving communities in decision making and the generation of culture. The Internet provides them with more ways to reach (new) audiences and to decouple their activities from the restraints of place and time. At the same time these institutions and the values that are embedded within them are under attack. This challenge comes in two different forms. In many countries, there is increasing pressure on the independence of these institutions by governments. In parallel, large commercial market players question the very logic of public provision of public goods and services in attempts to grow their own markets. As a result, the potential of public institutions and small and medium sized digital companies to uphold inclusivity, democracy, and equality of our societies in the digital age has been largely dormant; many of these institutions struggle to find their role in the digital environment.

> If we understand the Internet as a market-driven platform dominated by global conglomerates and not as a basic universal service and a public infrastructure, we abandon our ability to protect our democratic systems and to shield citizens from over-commodification.

Our current policies in the digital area fail to empower public institutions, and instead hold them back from innovation in the delivery of public services. Outdated and inflexible copyright laws are limiting research and education and prevent cultural heritage institutions from sharing their collections online. Public service broadcasters are reduced to continue providing linear programming that mimics the radio and television channels of the 20th century instead of developing online-first strategies that can challenge the attention-monopolies of social media platforms. Education and learning is confined to formal educational institutions instead of embedded in the fabric of everyday life.

The majority of these limitations are undertaken in order to "protect" the market from undue competition. Instead of envisioning the Internet as a true public space in which publicly funded institutions play an important and visible role as producers of content, they are confined to the margins. The lack of strategies for a digital transformation of public institutions means that we have largely surrendered the digital environment to the ever-increasing influence of commercial online platforms that erode our democratic values.

A Europe that seeks to develop its own position in the digital age that is true to its decades-old tradition of public institutions needs to empower these same institutions to provide meaningful services and to provide the public with shared online spaces that are protected from the surveillance practices of commercial platforms.

Instead of slowly eroding these institutions in the interest of an ever-expanding market sector, it is necessary to create strong public institutions that can compete with commercial platforms when it comes to access to information, knowledge, culture. Public institutions should take the lead in ensuring that our values and democracy can flourish in the digital age.

Towards a Shared Digital Europe

Combine these four elements with a truly European set of values and a new strategy presents itself. A strategy that understands the digital space as a hybrid space, both a market and a public space where the commons can also thrive. A strategy that policy makers and civil society actors can use to counter the current lack of democratic oversight in the digital space, the deteriorating online debate, the monopolisation of the digital sphere, the enclosure of knowledge and the means of knowledge production and the increasing violation of human rights in the digital space.

Most importantly our Vision for a Shared Digital Europe provides policy makers with an opportunity to work towards a truly European idea about how society should function in the digital age.

(This text is an abbreviated version of the vision published in April 2019 on https://shared-digital.eu)[1]

11. OWN THIS! A PORTFOLIO OF PLATFORM COOPERATIVISM, IN PROGRESS

Trebor Scholz

A Own This! A Portfolio of Platform Coopertivism, in Progress

by Trebor Scholz

Today, the power asymmetry between those who own the World Wide Web's core platforms and the users who depend on them, is more pronounced than ever. A decentralized digital economy is needed that is built on broad-based ownership and democratic governance. Platform Cooperativism could be an answer.

Platform capitalism, the economic system currently dominating the Internet, is not working for most people. Despite its initial promise as a new commons, the Internet now serves primarily the few, not the many.

First, the model has resulted in a broken social contract be-tween workers and businesses, exacerbating income inequality. Platforms like Airbnb and Uber focus on short-term returns and rapid growth to please investors, externalizing the risk of business to workers, while offering few essential benefits. Contract work and automation are replacing direct employment at every turn. Precariousness abounds. Second, platform capitalism exacerbates existing social inequities given that many gigs are performed by people who are invisible to customers. Persons of color, especially women of color, are seeing less pay, fewer benefits, and hardly any opportunity for meaningful on-the-job skills training. Many non-white and disabled platform users remain unprotected against discrimination, too. And third, we now live in an era of surveillance capitalism. Despite the fortunes of Silicon Valley investors and developers, the users who give actual value to platforms through their data do not co-govern them. The narrative that these platforms have ushered in a new era of "sharing" only obfuscates the real revolution: the monetization and capitalization of nearly every dimension of our lives, from dating to dishwashing. Despite their continued expansion, investor-backed capitalist platforms dominating today's Internet are not invincible. We have seen online empires collapse before: remember Yahoo, Lotus, Friend-ster, AOL, or MySpace? There is nothing inevitable about technological development.

In the face of widespread dissatisfaction with capitalism, and in the face of alarming income inequality driven increasingly by these capitalist platforms, it is time to collectively ask: 'What kind of new digital economy do we want to create?'

A Humane Alternative to the Winner-Takes-All Economy

Instead of optimizing the online economy for growth and short-term profits for the few, we need to optimize the online economy for workers and all people. Platform Cooperativism, as developed by Trebor Scholz and popularized by countless people around the world, chiefly Nathan Schneider, does this by applying the 200-year history of cooperatives – its lessons, principles, and best practices – to the digital economy.[1,2]

A cooperative is defined as an autonomous association of persons united voluntarily to meet their common economic, social, and cultural needs and aspirations through a jointly-owned and democratically-controlled enterprise. A platform is an online application or website used by individuals or groups to connect to one another or to organize services. Platform Co-operativism, the growing movement to cooperatize online businesses, builds on these values by establishing four key principles of its own:[3,4,5]

* Broad-based ownership, in which stakeholders and workers own, and therefore direct and control, the technological fea-tures, production processes, algorithms, data, job structures and all other aspects of their online platform.

* Democratic governance, in which all stakeholders and work-ers who own the platform collectively self-govern the entity through a one-person, one-vote principle.

* Co-design of the platform, in which various users and marginalized persons are included in the design and creation of the platform so that software is not pushed down onto users, but instead grows out of their needs, capacities, and aspirations.

* And, a commitment to open source development, so that platform co-ops can build new structures of collective ownership and democratic governance, while lifting up other emerging cooperatives in disparate locations, who can avoid having to reinvent the wheel, and apply the cooperative model through a commons of open source code.

Whichever way you look at them, platform co-ops place people at the center, and allow worker-owners to set their own objectives for business. Through distributed ownership, platform co-ops ground the digital economy democratically through a fundamentally new business model that, for the first time, puts workers and users ahead of profits and stockholders. This is not only a struggle for social justice. It is also a struggle for economic development. There have been also successful attempts of platform co-ops pushing back against the gig economy.[6,7]

Platform Co-ops Are Already Here

The platform co-op movement is not a figment of the academic imagination. The platform co-op movement is already here. It has gained momentum in numerous sectors and in numerous countries around the globe. The ecosystem of platform co-ops, some 240 projects currently, reaches from Brazil to Switzerland, India to Canada, East Asia to Africa, and places in between.[8,9,10] Various types of platform co-ops are developing and pushing into new markets against the status quo:

- Producer platform co-ops like Stocksy, and Resonate

- Worker platform co-ops like Green Taxi, Co-Rise, and Up & Go

- Data platform co-ops like MIDATA, and Social.coop

- And mutual risk co-ops like smart are proving the sustaina-bility and resiliency of the new business model.

Platform co-ops are ripe for interventions into additional industries, such as food delivery, trash pickup, elder care, short-term rental, transportation, data entry, child care, home repair, social media, higher education, and many others. Projects like Fairbnb, CoopCycle, and others are pushing into these sectors.

Workers value platform cooperatives too, because they offer several key benefits not available in the traditional "business-as-usual" approach of platform capitalism:

- Better job quality and security

- An inclusive design that respects workers needs

- Workers' formal inclusion in governance of the enterprise

- Value creation not just for workers, but for the community

Platform co-ops also exhibit greater productivity among workers, demonstrate greater resiliency in unsteady markets, and encourage workers to organize not just in the workplace, but in their communities and around larger political issues. Online tools like Loomio are emerging to help facilitate democratic governance for these businesses, accompanying the best practices emerging from existing platform co-ops. Finally, employee ownership, is a central component of cooperatives. Worker ownership is supported by both conservative and liberal political parties across continents.[11]

Platform co-ops offer a new vision for society. They are actually existing alternatives to some of our current economic dilemmas. The platform co-op movement offers a critical reform, but one that is also deeply structural. It is a reform that has the potential to fundamentally alter power relations in an enduring fashion. If one economic paradigm can slowly lose power through this reform, so too can its alternative gain power, building on small successes. This is the potential of the platform co-op movement.

12. DIGITAL COMMONING AND THE FIGHT FOR A HUMAN-CENTERED INTERNET

Mai Ishikawa Sutton

Digital Commoning and the Fight for a Human-Centered Internet

by Mai Ishikawa Sutton

It rarely gets hot out in San Francisco, but especially not in the peak of summer. You're much more likely to be engulfed by a cold fog than be graced by a single ray of sun. It was July 2018. I wrapped my coat tightly around myself and walked out of the Powell BART station onto the bustle of Market Street. I wasn't only bracing for the weather, but for the gut wrenching feeling I get when walking through this part of town.

On the sidewalk, chattering flocks of perky tech workers float by. To their left and right, downcast people look roughed up by the elements. On the bright green painted bike lanes, people zoom by on $1,500 Onewheel skateboards, dodging those who push all their possessions in a shopping cart. Shiny glass buildings tower over the realities of the people who live at street level. The homeless crisis has gotten so bad here that a UN official has called the conditions "shocking and intolerable."[1]

The Internet has taken the world by storm — transforming economies, societies, and politics. But the eye of this storm is the Bay Area, where the human cost of the tech boom is acutely experienced day-to-day. Here is where people invest billions of dollars in new apps, gadgets, and services. Here, smart people work overtime to build things that utterly transform the way people live. Yet in the midst of all this exertion, public infrastructure is crumbling and thousands of people have become unhoused. Even on the warmest days in San Francisco, the city has an air of indifference that is chilling.

This crisis of material human suffering shares its roots with the rise of human rights violations that pervade the internet, including mass corporate surveillance, the exploitation of personal data, and the censorship of online expression. These cases of neglect and exploitation are familiar because we see them happening in every part of the economy. They are by-products of capitalism — an ideology that justifies even the most harmful policies and practices for the growth and wealth of private firms. People are still grappling with the worst externalities of internet capitalism. Many activists are working hard to hold tech companies accountable and pass laws to stop their exploitative practices. Yet there are others who build alternatives. They are exploring how things could be better altogether by revolutionizing how we approach technology, innovation and the internet. These builders are looking at how we can move away from an internet that is based on profit, to an internet that is built on solidarity.

Internet of Profit

As one of the first generations of digital natives who grew up using the internet as a child, I've seen how it can be a source of joy and empowerment. It provides global spaces that allow us to share information and media that is beautiful, absurd, and heartbreaking. Memes and hashtags give us a common vocabulary to share our feelings and stories. The internet has become a critical platform for us to confront sexual assault, racism and hate. It has given people community. The global network of networks that we call the internet has triggered a worldwide exchange of ideas and creativity that is unprecedented.

But most of these positive aspects have come at a cost. Largely without our consent, we have become test subjects whose private data is harvested. Our data enables companies to manipulate our material needs and emotional desires. They condition us to become increasingly docile consumers, addicted to convenience and quantifiable fame and attention. We don't have to look far to see why the internet's worst elements are eclipsing the good.

> The wonderful things that the internet can provide are all too often outweighed by the abuses that are justified by capitalism.

Many of the worst human rights violations online can be directly attributed to for-profit corporations. Legally, they are obligated to maximize the wealth of those who own the companies. It says so in their bylaws, the legal contract that dictates their operations and objectives. These for-profit motives drive most social networks, hosting services and internet service providers (ISPs), to name just a few. As long as they are for-profit corporations, their primary focus must be to make money. Therefore it's usually only a matter of time before some aspect of their business violates human rights. The payoff — for instance, to exploit personal data — is too great, while the consequences for their actions are often negligible. The wonderful things that the internet can provide are thus all too often outweighed by the abuses that are justified by capitalism.

Violations to our privacy and freedom of expression are common in this internet of profit. However, I'd like to point to a few other harmful externalities that have also gotten recent attention.

Worker Disempowerment

As users are exploited, the workers who build and maintain internet services are too. The maltreatment of Uber drivers, Deliveroo riders and the rest of the contingent workforce is rampant, while companies pamper those higher up in the chain. High salaries, free meals and excellent social benefits are a norm among those in the tech workforce elite. But even these coddled workers are locked into highly managed hierarchies — with the shareholders at the top, the board of directors is under them, then the CEO, and a long line of managers overseeing everyone else. Each is beholden to their superiors. No one is to prioritize the well-being of their colleagues, the users of their product, or even themselves — except for those shareholders who'll someday profit off the whole operation.

Violating Net Neutrality

Net neutrality would not be an issue if internet service providers (ISPs) could not profit handsomely by discriminating between different types of content they serve to subscribers. But they can. Without net neutrality, companies can therefore be free to charge more for certain types of access. Legal protections for users can prevent ISPs from limiting who can see what on the internet based on what they can afford. Net neutrality regulations are urgent and required to protect the free and open internet because ISPs are much too inclined to squeeze their subscribers for extra monetary fees.

Environmental Externalities

The cell phones we carry in our pockets, the laptops we use for work — all of these networked devices contain a wide range of toxic minerals that are extracted from the Earth. For instance, most rechargeable lithium ion batteries contain cobalt from the Congo, obtained by people under hazardous conditions.[2] While some effort has been made by EU lawmakers to curb the human rights violations associated with the manufacturing of our internet-enabled products, it is still far from enough.[3]

> The cell phones we carry in our pockets, the laptops we use for work — all of these networked devices contain a wide range of toxic minerals that are extracted from the Earth.

Meanwhile, companies do little to nothing to make devices last longer than a few years. Longer-lasting devices would lead to falling sales. Apple does everything in its power to make it more difficult to repair parts on their phones.[4] These devices are treated as disposable, enabling widespread neglect of the human and environmental costs involved in building them.

Undermining Democracy

As is common practice among large corporate firms, tech companies are not shy about throwing around their resources to influence government policies. In the EU, they have quickly risen to become one of the most powerful industry blocs to lobby their way through Brussels. Airbnb and Uber are infamous examples.[5,6,7] They spend millions of dollars at local city elections in the U.S. and the EU to stop regulations that would adversely affect their business, even when the laws are designed for the public interest.[8]

Multinational technology companies are also actively undermining national governments through international law. Tech companies are influencing trade agreements to win favorable terms, framing data as a commodity that must flow freely across borders.[9] Even constraints on how data is collected and shared between companies, such as to protect user privacy, are framed by industry representatives as a trade barrier that must be stopped.

This internet, built out of profit-seeking organizations, is unhealthy. It is disempowering, restrictive, and environmentally unsustainable. What if — instead of the internet being built out of profit — it were built out of solidarity?

> As is common practice among large corporate firms, tech companies are not shy about throwing around their resources to influence government policies.

Internet of Solidarity

The commons is often mistaken to be a passive shared resource that is used and easily exploitable by people. But it's not. The commons is an economic and social paradigm that is fundamentally about prioritizing solidarity. In a commons, the resource is a shared problem that invites our collective concern. It provides an opportunity for people to have better relationships with each other by caring about the same thing. This expands our empathy and encourages better communication. Instead of being competitors in a struggle for artifically scarce resources, it inspires us to see each other as neighbors, as equal collaborators for survival.

Internet services and platforms can prioritize collective human empowerment. In an ideal world, they would be fully committed to it, both legally and culturally. They would have to institutionalize participatory and inclusive governance. Direct democracy, representative democracy, and sortition are only a few examples of ways that internet-based companies could be run as a commons. These decision-making models are usually exercised in government, but they can also be applied to companies — namely, cooperatives. There are many well-known examples of internet commons projects, such as Wikipedia, the Internet Archive, the Tor Network. But there are still many legal, political and economic challenges that prevent such commons from emerging or thriving in the current world.

To shed light on some other types of internet commoning, I'll share a few examples. Even though they do not fully embrace the commons concept, in their own way these projects address one of the problems of the internet of profit as explained above. They point us toward what an internet of solidarity may look like.

Worker Empowerment

New movements are emerging to make tech companies more accountable to their workers. Platform cooperativism is a movement to shift ownership and control over internet platforms from managers and shareholders to its workers and users. The thinking is to democratize the governance over these platforms and expand their priorities to encompass a wider array of issues concerning the community. Tech Workers Coalition is a group organizing to improve the working conditions of those in the tech industry.[10] They are active in working to hold their companies accountable for projects that undermine human rights or are otherwise ethically misguided.

Protecting Net Neutrality

If ISP subscribers owned and controlled their own last-mile internet infrastructure, then they would likely decide not to throttle their connections or raise monthly subscription prices. A community network is one that is built and operated by the people who use it. It's not about extracting profit. It's about providing a service that's best for its user-owners, and that includes making it inexpensive for them to connect to the internet. A report published by the Internet Society and Centre for European Policy Studies explored five case studies of community-owned networks across Europe.[11] It concluded that such networks could help bridge the digital divide by providing affordable connections to people in remote areas.

Environmental Sustainability

The source and method of mineral extraction to build our devices is an immense design challenge that must be grappled with. In the shorter term however, we must find ways to make technology less disposable. iFixit is an online community manual for people to share information and methods to repair broken things.[12] It is a for-profit company that manages the website and sells tools and parts to repair common devices, such as iPhones. While it is for-profit, the iFixit platform is in many ways a commons, where the members write and share high-quality repair instructions.

Strengthening Democracy

There have been many projects to strengthen democratic processes, particularly in the U.S. following the 2016 Presidential election. However, there are some older projects that have worked for several years to expand government transparency and open democratic deliberation. Public. Resource.Org digitizes and makes accessible works of the United States Federal Government which are not available online.[13] Major projects conducted by the organization include the digitizing and sharing of large numbers of court records, U.S. government-produced video, and laws. Loomio is used by hundreds of cooperatives and organizations worldwide, including within circles of Podemos in Spain.[14] Essentially, it's a tool for collective deliberation and asynchronous decisionmaking. Loomio provides options for different types of voting, such as a poll, ranked choice, or saying yes or no to a given proposal.

An internet that is based on solidarity would not violate our human rights to the extent that our current internet does today. Organizations that inherently care about their workers, community members, and their impact on the world would have to build human rights protections into their services. This becomes much easier to do when you do not have to make constant trade-offs in the name of profit.

Digital Commons and Human Rights

We have so much to do to fix the internet itself. However, much of it will also be impacted by extreme, foreseeable changes to our life here on Earth. As we forge ahead through the Anthropocene, it's critical that we use networked communication to share information and media that will help us face these future challenges. We don't have time to waste dealing with internet platforms that embolden powerful actors, censor the marginalized, and boost lies over truth.

The promise of a commons-based internet is to communicate and share information in the best possible way. When platforms and services are governed democratically, it helps us choose what works for our community and our individual needs. It's the same with food, water, air, or housing — we have to be able to talk through what works, what doesn't, and what needs to be done to protect ourselves and the shared resource. To commonify the internet is not an end in itself, but a stepping stone, making it easier for us to turn everything we need to survive and thrive on this planet into a commons.

The Bay Area has in many ways become a dystopian reality. It is one of the many grim truths of this global tech boom. But this must not become an accepted fact nor be discounted as an unavoidable negative externality of this business. Networked technologies do not need to plunge us into a world of growing detachment and indifference. Let's recognize that the most valuable kind of innovation is that which expands our ability to flourish as a species. We can be empathetic, trusting, and helpful to each other. The internet should help make us better people. If it's not going to bring out the best of humanity, what's the point?

> Let's recognize that the most valuable kind of innovation is that which expands our ability to flourish as a species. We can be empathetic, trusting, and helpful to each other. The internet should help make us better people. If it's not going to bring out the best of humanity, what's the point?

Policymakers, innovators, organizers, and everyone else can take part in bringing about the internet of solidarity. First of all, it needs to become much less appealing to start or operate for-profit businesses. Policymakers could stop generous tax breaks to for-profit tech companies and break up the platform monopolies using antitrust laws (as some officials are actively seeking to do). They could enact financial incentives for commons-based projects to get off the ground. This might take the form of public investment in platform cooperatives or generous tax breaks for business-to-coop conversions. With public support in place, it would make it people to take risks and try their hand at building new commons-based internet start-ups. We need the same kind of bold experimentation that occurs among for-profit tech start-ups to build organizations that could someday be viable not-for-profit alternatives to the exploitative services we use today.

This will all be a huge undertaking. None of this is possible if we go on believing that we are better off only serving our own self interests. But I am optimistic. I believe that humans have an incredible untapped capacity to empathize and work together with others, that we can choose to do that instead of putting all our energy and belief in unsustainable, wealth-seeking corporations. This is what it means to build up the commons. We need to work with each other, for each other, to build up shared public resources and infrastructure. It will take considerable shift in our thinking, but thankfully, we have leaders like those in this book who are showing us the way.

13. FROM LAB TO COMMONS: HEALTH AS A COMMON GOOD

Sophie Bloemen

From Lab to Commons:
Health as a Common Good

by Sophie Bloemen

From the 15th century until the 20th century, powerful people all over the world enclosed and privatized commonly-held land. Up until then, this land was owned and managed by local communities. This process displaced hundreds of millions of farmers who lost their autonomous means of sustenance and were forcibly cast into urban labour markets.

In the late 20th century and early 21st century, a similar movement took place. This time, it enclosed the public good of scientific knowledge and technology. Aided by intellectual property laws, transnational treaties, regulatory capture and international trade agreements, the enclosure movement turned knowledge into privatized products.

Problems and limitations of the current model

Although the current biomedical system has produced important lifesaving treatments, billions of people around the world cannot afford these medicines, resulting in over 10 million preventable deaths each year. Research and Development (R&D) priorities are not determined by public health needs but by market incentives.

This is the result of an ineffective and costly R&D system that turns new medicines into monopolies, using patent protection. It has allowed companies to set exorbitant prices, draining public health resources and excluding many patient from accessing treatments. The enclosure of knowledge impedes collaboration and leads to an overall lack of transparency. Thriving on secrecy and geared towards profits, this system stifles innovation. It leads to skyrocketing costs, over-diagnosis, over-prescription and the medicalization of health. Together with our overall market-oriented system this has led to privatizing of biomedical knowledge as well as the commodification and commercialisation of health.

A large part of the investment in medical knowledge comes from public funding. The public sector plays a crucial role in funding high-risk research. It is estimated that public funding accounts for 30 to 65 percent of global R&D costs. Many medicines were not only researched but also developed with public money. Finally, we use public funds to pay for those medicines once they are on the market.

Exclusion coming home

The current pharmaceutical business model has long excluded people in the Global south from the fruits of science. It deemed many treatments unaffordable for most people outside of Europe or the US. Little research and investment has gone into diseases that do not have a profitable market potential. This is why they are called 'neglected diseases'. In reality, it is the patients, the people who are neglected.

Skyrocketing prices are also starting to threaten access to medicines in European countries, creating massive financial stress on public health systems. An increasing number of treatments for life threatening diseases such as cancer and hepatitis C are unaffordable for both individuals and national health systems, especially in Eastern Europe. Governments are forced to make devilish choices between people: they simply cannot treat everyone.

Winds of Change

A consensus of dissatisfaction with the present health innovation system has developed over the last years within the public health community. The need for change is obvious; policy makers, researchers, health practitioners and patients are aware something needs to happen. There is a growing willingness to address today's encroachment on the Right to Health in the biomedical sector, but where would we begin transforming a complex and entrenched system?

> Little research and investment has gone into diseases that do not have a profitable market potential. This is why they are called 'neglected diseases'. In reality, it is the patients, the people who are neglected.

Ensuring people's access to affordable treatments has not been a policy priority. Instead, policy has been almost exclusively geared towards the growth of European economies and maximization of profits. Many governments are now demanding more transparency and taking actions to bargain harder with pharma in price negotiations. The Netherlands has given this movement a significant push during their EU presidency, questioning the current Intellectual Property system. Yet the push-back from vested interests has been overwhelming. Biomedical policy needs a true paradigm shift in order to support a health innovation system that is productive, affordable, accessible and democratic.

A vision for the future: embracing the commons

How can we move towards as system that embraces health as a common good? How can we take a truly public interest approach to biomedical innovation, driven by health needs? Today there is a loud call for a biomedical innovation system that produces public value and stimulates collaboration, a model that manages knowledge and patents in a beneficial way. A wide variety of voices are questioning whether monopolies on medicines were such a great idea after all.

The commons are an important piece of the puzzle. They teach us to share essential resources, bolstering equity and sustainability. Instead of extracting and enclosing resources for private use, the commons show us how to create an abundance of immaterial knowledge while wisely governing scarce natural resources.

Little by little they are becoming part of the discourse and the lens through which issues around biomedical innovation and access to medicines are considered. People are discussing shared ownership, democratic governance, decentralization, collective responsibility for health and efficient innovation through collaborative innovation and sharing knowledge. The idea of medicines as common goods rather than products is making inroads. As we can see in the essays on DNDi and the Medicines Patent Pool on the next pages, the idea of the commons informs and surfaces in biomedical innovation on different levels and aspects.

Guiding Principles

When we consider health as a common good and we want to manage it as a commons, it implies we should manage it in a democratic, public and equitable manner. We should strive to make sure everyone has access to the treatments they need. Taking this approach leads us to a number of guiding principles.

Although here we discuss medicines and the need for access to treatment, we should realise that market dynamics have led to a medicalization of health and we are presented with technological fixes for almost all our problems. Yet there is obviously no pill for every ill and a holistic approach to health leads us to be **wary of technological solutionism**.

On top of this, in order to take such a structural approach that looks at the system as a whole, we have to move **beyond solely individual rights** in our conception of social justice. A rights approach represents an individual claim to certain goods or freedoms. Yet we have to consider how these goods or resources are created in the first place and what we prioritize. So, additionally we should look at the collective interest and the **collective responsibility** for the governance of health and the provision of common goods.

Today we have a '**tragedy of the anti-commons**', the biomedical model is not failing society because it is a commons which has become overused. It is the opposite: a model with artificial scarcity of immaterial knowledge goods that are by their very nature abundant and shareable. Intellectual property rights restrict this sharing. This is due to a market structured to favour private, corporate interests. Instead, we should look at ways to **manage biomedical knowledge as a commons** and facilitate equitable access, collaborative innovation and democratic governance of the knowledge.

Managing knowledge as a commons is related to **open innovation** (Open access, open data, open source software). There is however an important distinction to be made between unregulated openness and the commons. 'Open' varies in practice. Placing knowledge in a commons does not just mean sharing data and knowledge without regard for their social use, access and preservation. It means introducing a **set of democratic rules and limits to assure equitable and sustainable sharing** for health related resources.

> Today we have a 'tragedy of the anti-commons', the biomedical model is not failing society because it is a commons which has become overused. It is the opposite: a model with artificial scarcity of immaterial knowledge goods that are by their very nature abundant and shareable.

The modes of production, both of knowledge, scientific process and physical products, should be generative rather than extractive, avoiding the waste, duplication and opacity of our present model. Their governance can be understood as a type of stewardship – in the sense of the responsible and careful management of entrusted resources.

Knowledge commons could facilitate open global research and local production adapted to local contexts (see DNDI example in chapter 15). Attention for the collective and the democratic management of knowledge also translates to an awareness of community and social localised ecosystems. The saying, *nothing about us, without us,* used by HIV/AIDS patient activists who claimed a say in policies and decisions about treatment in the 1990s, is still as relevant as ever. Democratic governances and shared ownership not only serve the development of better, suitable, appropriate treatments for different populations. Creating local capacity to develop and produce medicines eventually serves sustainable access to treatment as well.

Finally, there is an **important role for institutions to support the biomedical commons** and forge public-civic collaborations.

Transitional and transformational Initiatives

How can we begin transforming such a complex system? How to move away from the centralised and commercialised practices around health? First we have to let go of the idea that there is no alternative to the current system. Of course there is, there are many, we just have to envision, explore and build them.

We need to build on the many initiatives and approaches that are already helping to transition away from today's broken system. These initiatives include the use of open knowledge and collaborative innovation, as well as the use of incentive systems where intellectual property does not establish a barrier to access or use while innovators are still rewarded. Some of the key approaches are the following:

- In order to truly move to another system, we have to move away from the expectation of high prices to stimulate investment in R&D as is now the case. The patent provides for temporary market exclusivity, in other words: a monopoly. Moving away from that means de-linking investment in R&D from the expectation of high prices. This means giving monetary rewards other than through monopolies, for example through innovation prizes.

- This allows for the sharing of knowledge, instead of privatising it, generic production and affordable access to the medicines. Some initiatives seek to protect knowledge as a public good through public interest licensing of public research results, and open data policies. Reshaping the incentive system also allows for shifting incentives towards needs driven innovation and added therapeutic benefit.

- Data commons for biomedical R&D are a shared virtual space where scientists can work with the digital objects of biomedical research such as data and analytical tools. One could imagine building a science commons infrastructure of repositories.

- Patent pools are classical knowledge commons where there is institutionalised governance of knowledge and or data. The Medicines patent pool is a UN backed public health organisation working to increase access to HIV, Hepatitis C and tuberculosis treatment in low and middle-income countries. Working with industry, governments and patients and other stakeholders, it licenses needed medicines. It manages knowledge as a commons by pooling the IP, which accelerates innovation and provides affordable access though generic competition.

- Product Development Partnerships are non-profit organisations that develop affordable, innovative medicines for neglected patients and diseases. DNDi is an example of such a non-profit medicines developer.

- Some existing initiatives follow the lead of other sectors experimenting with open source and decentralized production, like bio Hack labs and peer-to-peer cooperatives. Open source is a concept that stems from software development and involves open data sharing, collaboration and results sharing. The worldwide open source community insists on the possibility of participation in a project by anyone in real time and a form of shared ownership that ensures the underlying method and data are public domain.

- The Do-It-Yourself Biology (DIYbio) community applies open source working methods and is emerging as a movement that fosters open access to resources permitting modern molecular biology, and synthetic biology among others. Since 2010, community labs started opening up and became embodiments of the nascent DIYbio community, a grassroots movement of enthusiasts seeking to popularize and democratize biotechnology.

What we see in all these initiatives is the move towards decommodifying medicines and a democratising governance and ownership.

What about policy?

EU member states and institutions can ensure the stewardship of health by ushering in a more democratic, affordable and sustainable biomedical system. What are polices that transition society away from the current proprietary and centralised model?

A central element of our current system is the intellectual property rights management and this needs to be reformed. Perverse incentives should be take out. It can be done gradually. At the same time investment in alternative models is needed.

Overall institutional ecology will have to be adapted to support bottom up developments and move away from the current centralized model with a few big players to a more decentralized model where knowledge is shared. This will require regulatory reform and investments.

Policies can build on the transitional initiatives and approaches such as open science and bringing knowledge in public ownership. It will be important to enable democratic governance of knowledge; for instance making sure data are shared and ensuring transparency for reliable evidence of health care decisions. It will also require directing trade policy toward creating public goods, and embracing trade policies that open up instead of enclose biomedical knowledge and technology transfer to the Global South.

These are the main directions. We need to approach biomedical innovation less as a profit making opportunity and more like a essential public health issue. Seeing health as commons puts forth a vision of collective benefit pertinent to European citizens in their current circumstances. It also puts forward a practical approach to managing knowledge with multiple benefits. New technologies are facilitating new forms of knowledge production and medicine development outside of the current dominant model. These new developments are starting to take root and they need to be nurtured and supported by financial and regulatory frameworks.

The European Commission and the member states should explore, support and guide initiatives which have the potential of transforming our present biomedical innovation model in favour of the common good. European policy makers, civil society organizations, health-care professionals and citizens will all be crucial to the process of negotiating a transition from the today's deficient market-driven biomedical model to a model designed to serve universal health needs.

This text is based on the Commons Network policy paper 'From Lab to Commons' (2018) by Sophie Bloemen, David Hammerstein and contributing author Carolyn Whitten.

14. THE MEDICINES PATENT POOL: A REMEDY FOR THE ANTI-COMMONS

Ellen 't Hoen

The Medicines Patent Pool: A Remedy for the Anti-Commons

by Ellen 't Hoen

In 2002, at the International AIDS Conference in Barcelona, a group of people met in a small meeting room to discuss the high prices of antiretroviral medicines (ARVs) for the treatment of HIV/AIDS.

In those days, generic, non-patented ARVs were much lower priced and available from companies in India, as they were not barred from producing these medicines because India did not grant product patents for medicines. But this was going to change. The World Trade Organization's rules demanded that India be compliant with the global Agreement on Trade-Related Aspects of Intellectual Property Rights — the TRIPS Agreement. As a result, India would have to grant medicines patents from 2015 on. At the same time, newer and more robust medicines had started to become available in wealthier nations at high prices. Concerns were growing about how these new treatments could be made available in easy-to-use three-in-one pills in the absence of generic production.

To the surprise of the audience in Barcelona, Knowledge Ecology International's Director James Love put up a picture of the patent application for an early 20th century airplane.[1] The early developers of the airplane held patents on the technology. They were not keen to share their technology and took legal action whenever they suspected infringement of their patents. But these patent wars were really starting to hamper the United States' ability to develop and produce military airplanes. The government had to intervene and so established the first government mandated patent pool in which all airplane producers were required to collaborate.[2]

"If we can do this for reasons of war, why can't we do this to fight HIV/AIDS?" This was the question James Love put to the group at the AIDS conference. He outlined how the intellectual property needed for the production of low-cost AIDS/HIV medicines could be brought together in a patent pool for any eligible generic producer to use. This would not only guarantee the production of low cost medicines but also take away barriers to putting different compounds together in one pill and develop adapted formulations, such as those needed to treat children.

In such a pooling scheme, a generic producer would be allowed to make use of the patent in exchange for a royalty payment to the patent holder. This meant that patents would no longer pose a barrier to the production and supply of generic medicines, just like it was before the TRIPS Agreement. Just as the flying machine pool made large-scale production of military airplanes possible, so would a mandated medicines patent pool enable large-scale generic production of life-saving medicines. It was a brilliant idea. The question was how to implement it.

Winds of Change

In 2006, a new global health financing mechanism, called UNITAID, had been established by a group of countries. Its mission was manifold: to scale up access to treatment for HIV/AIDS, tuberculosis, and malaria, achieve price reductions for medicines that meet international quality standards and diagnostics, and accelerate availability of medicines. What set UNITAID apart from other donors at that time was its clear mandate to work on intellectual property issues related to access to medicines.

UNITAID's constitution specifically demanded the organisation to support the World Trade Organization Doha Declaration on TRIPS and Public Health. The Doha Declaration was adopted in 2001 and stated that the TRIPS Agreement does not stand in the way of measures needed to protect public health, thereby introducing the primacy of health over trade considerations. The Declaration further outlined measures countries can take when patents form a barrier to ensure access to medicines for all, and suspended the obligation of least developed countries to provide or enforce medicines product patents.[3] Further, UNITAID was open to new and innovative ideas to tackle medicine access problems and showed leadership in taking on promising, yet controversial proposals.

> The principle of a patent pool is to facilitate the availability of new technologies by making patents and other forms of intellectual property more readily available to entities other than the patent holder. The pool is intended to avert a "tragedy of the anti-commons" in which people are unable to make use of knowledge because of the entanglement of property rights that block them.

Also, in 2006, the World Health Organization Commission on Intellectual Property Rights, Innovation and Public health (CIPIH) recommended the establishment of a patent pool.[4] These developments strengthened the resolve of Knowledge Ecology International and Médecins sans Frontières in proposing to UNITAID to establish a medicines patent pool.

The principle of a patent pool is to facilitate the availability of new technologies by making patents and other forms of intellectual property more readily available to entities other than the patent holder. The pool is intended to avert a "tragedy of the anti-commons" in which people are unable to make use of knowledge because of the entanglement of property rights that block them.[5]

Patent pools have been established in various fields related to public health — examples include the Golden Rice in agriculture, a vaccine for Severe Acute Respiratory Syndrome (SARS), as well as multiple areas of information technology. The aim of all of those initiatives was to overcome barriers to access and innovation that may arise when relevant patents are owned by many different entities.[6,7]

The UNITAID Patent Pool, as it was called in the early days, was a new idea. It focused on medicines and the collective management of pharmaceutical patents and other intellectual property for the purpose of accelerating access to medical innovations in low- and middle-income countries. The purpose of the UNITAID initiative was first and foremost to serve the public interest by creating the collective management of intellectual property related to important life-saving medicines. In essence, it transferred control over intellectual property from corporations to the larger community, making sure that all people had access to proper treatment.

After a feasibility study that concluded that the proposal was indeed desirable and doable, UNITAID formed an in-house team to develop an implementation plan for the Medicines Patent Pool (MPP) in 2009.[8] A year later, in 2010, the Medicines Patent Pool was established as a separate legal entity and opened its doors in Geneva. UNITAID would remain its core funder until this day.

> The purpose was to serve the public interest by creating the collective management of intellectual property related to important life-saving medicines. In essence, it transferred control over intellectual property from corporations to the larger community, making sure that all people had access to proper treatment.

In the early days, not all players in the global health arena were keen on the Medicines Patent Pool. Opposition came from unexpected corners such as the Bill and Melinda Gates Foundation, which was a member of the UNITAID board. They initially refused to support the establishment of the Medicines Patent Pool. The Gates' fortune mainly derived from Microsoft's intellectual property, which is possibly why the Foundation was reluctant to support the idea.

The WHO leadership was also reluctant to embrace the initiative for fear it would fail. They insisted it be set up as a separate legal entity and not be housed at the WHO to avoid any potential liability issues. Certain factions of civil society saw the pool as not going far enough. Some claimed it would undermine other efforts to reform the system of intellectual property. Others expressed concern that the licenses from the pool might cover people in the poorest countries, but if they didn't cover people in all middle-income countries, those patients would be out of options.[9]

The key to the pool's success would be the willingness of patent holders, mostly pharmaceutical corporations, to engage and license their intellectual property. This was no small order considering that medicines patents are the crown jewels of the industry. It would not be easy to persuade them to part with them. Some in the industry responded to the establishment of the patent pool idea with resistance. For example, one company told the Financial Times that they could better accelerate access themselves and that "The pool's key focus has been political in getting access to IP without explaining how it will work. [...] The 4.7m they will spend could save thousands of lives [by buying drugs.]"[10]

Other companies were more forthcoming in the early days. Gilead was notable in that it publicly declared at the 2008 AIDS conference to be open to licensing its intellectual property to the Medicines Patent Pool.

> The key to the pool's success would be the willingness of patent holders, mostly pharmaceutical corporations, to engage and license their intellectual property. This was no small order considering that medicines patents are the crown jewels of the industry.

A first breakthrough for the Pool came when the US National Institutes for Health (NIH) approached UNITAID and offered to license its patents related to HIV medications. In 2010, the Medicines Patent Pool signed its first agreement with NIH.[11] It became apparent that this move had support from the highest political levels when the White House's blog encouraged companies to follow suit and congratulated those that did.[12,13,14,15] Gilead, an important holder of patents on essential and new medicines for the treatment of HIV, followed soon after. The company signed its first license agreement with the Medicines Patent Pool in 2011.[16] That same year, the first generic companies joined the initiative, which was crucial because generic companies are the ones that actually produce and sell low-priced medicines.[17]

Core features of the Medicines Patent Pool

The Medicines Patent Pool is "public health driven", not driven by the commercial needs of the companies with which it works. It focuses on essential products and areas of greatest health need. Its country scope is low- and middle-income countries, which means that it seeks to include as many countries as possible in the scope of the licenses. The country scope is one of the great challenges for the Medicines Patent Pool because pharmaceutical companies do not like to give up large emerging markets such as Brazil, China, and Russia to their competitors.

Contrary to the airplane patent pool, which was a non-voluntary mechanism mandated by the government, the MPP was set up as a voluntary mechanism. This means that its success depended on the willingness of companies to part with full control over their intellectual property. A key feature of the Pool is that the licenses allow for multiple non-exclusive sub-licenses. This enables competition between generic manufactures which helps to drive down the price. The licenses also facilitate further innovation by allowing the development of new "three-in-one pills" or fixed-dose combinations (FDCs) and other products to treat children.

Another important feature of the MPP is that its work has to be consistent with the WTO Doha Declaration on TRIPS and Public Health. This means that the Pool cannot enter into agreements containing terms and conditions that limit the policy space countries have under international law, such as using compulsory licensing of medicines patents. As a result, the Medicines Patent Pool licenses allow the generic companies to supply generic medicines to countries that are not listed in the agreement when such countries make use of TRIPS flexibilities such as compulsory licensing.[18] If the Pool's licenses would not allow the generic companies they work with to supply to countries that have issued a compulsory license, the Pool could potentially paralyse the effectiveness of such measures.

The Pool's license agreements also include waivers for data exclusivity and require quality assurances of the medicines. When needed, the agreements can also provide for technology transfer. A significant and unique feature is the transparency of the MPP's licenses. They all are available, in full text, on the MPP's website.[19]

State of play today

Today, the Medicines Patent Pool has licenses from nine companies related to 18 products. All of the standard first- and second- line treatments for HIV/AIDS, as recommended by the WHO, are covered by licenses in the MPP. The MPP includes licenses needed to produce a medicine for the treatment of hepatitis C and also one for tuberculosis.

A total of 24 generic companies and drug developers have licensed from the Patent Pool. As a result, there are over 130 drug development projects that are ongoing. The Pool licenses for HIV/AIDS drugs cover between 92 and 131 countries. This means that between 87% and 91% of adults with HIV/AIDS, and 100% of children, can benefit from the MPP.

The new first-line HIV treatment, TLD (tenofovir/lamivudine/dolutegravir), was first developed by licensees of the MPP.[20] The generic company, Mylan, was the first to obtain marketing approval for the product in 2017, bringing a truly innovative product to market as a generic from the first day of sale.

The MPP also has three hepatitis C related licenses. The product licenses' territory ranges from 95 to 112 countries representing 47.5% to 65.4 % of people with hepatitis C. From 2012 to 2017, the Pool has created US $553 million in savings. In 2018, the board of the MPP expanded its mandate to all patented essential medicines.

> A total of 24 generic companies and drug developers have licensed from the Patent Pool. As a result, there are over 130 drug development projects that are ongoing. The Pool licenses for HIV/AIDS drugs cover between 92 and 131 countries. This means that between 87% and 91% of adults with HIV/AIDS, and 100% of children, can benefit from the MPP.

Conclusion

The Patent Pool's achievements are significant for an initiative that, only nine years ago, was regarded by many in the global health and trade arena as high risk and likely to fail. Of course, an element of self-interest of donor countries contributed to its success. Those countries wanted to make sure that finite global health financing for medicines was not spent on high-priced branded medicines which would have severely restricted the number of people that could be treated with the same amount of money.

It is therefore uncertain whether there will be enough political support for a similar voluntary licensing schemes for non-communicable diseases like cancer, diabetes, and asthma. Currently, national governments pay most of the costs of treatment for such diseases. It is therefore important that those governments become more vocal on the need for MPP licenses for medicines for non-communicable diseases. It is encouraging that some companies have signalled to be willing to work with the Patent Pool on cancer medication.[21]

The Pool has successfully pried some of the hold over medicines intellectual property, mostly related to HIV and hepatitis C products, away from the industry and put it to work for the public interest. However, the work of the Patent Pool did not stretch out to all middle-income countries, and is so far limited to a set of communicable diseases. Today's global struggle to lower prices for other medicines shows that it is vital that governments retain the right and ability to make corrections in the management of intellectual property of companies. This is especially true when such management leads to undesirable societal effects and does not serve the public interest.

15. DEVELOPING INNOVATIVE DRUGS THROUGH THE COMMONS: LESSONS FROM THE DNDI EXPERIENCE

Benjamin Coriat, Philippe Abecassis, Jean-Francois Alesandrini, Nathalie Coutinet and Stéphanie Leyronas

Developing Innovative Drugs Through the Commons: Lessons from the DNDi Experience

by Benjamin Coriat, Philippe Abecassis, Jean-Francois Alesandrini, Nathalie Coutinet and Stéphanie Leyronas

In this paper we argue that DNDi, even though it belongs to the family of Product Development Partnerships (PDPs) created at the end of the 20th century, has followed a very particular trajectory, that allows us to characterize it as a distinctive commons in the field of public health. We illustrate this view by focusing on two features: DNDi's promotion of collaborative platforms and its innovative intellectual property policy.

From PDP to Commons: DNDi's trajectory

To fully understand the significance of the DNDi project, it is necessary to look back at the end of the 20th century. This period saw heated international debate on the developing world's shortcomings in the availability of and access to care.[1] A distressing imbalance in the supply of drugs became clear: 90% of research and development (R&D) was conducted for the benefit of the 10% most wealthy and credit-worthy patients.[2] This concern was fuelled by the sudden tightening of Intellectual Property (IP) standards following the signature of the Trade-Related Aspects of the Intellectual Property Rights (TRIPS) Agreement in 1994.[3] The changes set up by the TRIPS Agreement included the compulsory patenting of therapeutic molecules in all signatory countries, thus creating a unified global market for patented drugs regardless of countries' levels of development.[4]

This setting gave rise to a series of institutional innovations to transform the fight against neglected diseases. These innovations especially converged under the form of Product Development Partnerships (PDPs), themselves largely based on new open innovation concepts.[5] These PDPs can be described as not-for-profit organisations dedicated to promoting the development of R&D in the field of neglected diseases. The first PDPs created for R&D in neglected diseases were the International Aids Vaccine Initiative (IAVI) and Medicines for Malaria Venture (MMV). They were followed by PDPs that mostly focused on medical products (vaccines, diagnostics, drugs, microbicides, etc.).

DNDi was part of this second wave of PDPs, but also showed unique characteristics. This distinctiveness makes its analysis through the lens of commons – rather than that of PDPs – particularly insightful.

The Shift from Global Public Goods to Commons and its Relevance in Understanding DNDi

Before reviewing some of the main features of DNDi through the lens of the commons, some insights are needed on the commons approach, especially as an alternative to the narrative on Global Public Goods (GPGs) that until recently was dominant regarding public health.

GPGs were introduced at the end of the 20th century as a broadened understanding of public goods within the traditional neoclassical framework.[6] Along with the archetypal GPGs – air, atmosphere, water – public health was often described as a GPG. After two to three decades, the GPGs approach has given way to a number of limitations and critiques, mainly that it perpetuates the standard economic vision based on the defense of property rights and efficiency.[7,8]

> The goal is first to support clinical research and then to facilitate the access of treatment for the greatest number of people, especially the most vulnerable populations.

The commons approach sets quite a different perspective. It questions the very roots of the GPGs approach, which focuses almost exclusively on regulations in a world seen as governed by agents in pursuit of private interests. While it does not exclude at all the need for appropriate regulations, the commons approach attaches at least equal importance to the establishment of local, decentralised and largely self-organised entities.

To be qualified as a commons, an organisation or institution should ideally combine three characteristics: i) they bring together, around an existing resource - and/or in view of producing a new resource - a group of self-organised actors that have committed themselves to some forms of sharing of the resource's use or creation ("shared resource"); ii) they allocate to the various actors a set of rights and obligations regarding the way in which the resource shall be treated and its benefits shared ("rules"); and iii) they establish forms of governance to promote the compliance with these rights and obligations ("governance").[9] Commons that meet these criteria come in various forms based on their goals and the nature of their institutional arrangements.

In addition to these formal characteristics of commons, two moral and political considerations conceived from the outset as an intrinsic part of their identity ought to be highlighted. First, the ecology of the system considered is at the very core of the construction of a commons: the rules implemented by commoners must therefore target the reproduction or joint enrichment of the resource and the community around it.[10] Second, equity is key. It is ensured by governance in the case of commons formed from exhaustible resources and characterized by universal access in the case of commons that are not rival and not exhaustible such as intangible goods or knowledge.

Based on these definitions, we argue that while DNDi does belong to the large PDP's family, it presents several distinctive features that render its analysis through the lens of commons relevant and powerful. Beyond its own governance and funding mechanisms that very much echo a multi-partner-based commons model, two of its characteristics will be further explored here: its promotion of collaborative platforms and intellectual property policy.

Collaborative Platforms conceived as commons-based innovative entities

A good illustration of DNDi's philosophy is the collaborative clinical research platforms set up, once a candidate molecule has been identified. The platforms provide a network of medical and scientific skills to promote a common approach for health authorities in endemic countries, as well as to define R&D priorities and product profile of drugs (i.e. main characteristics on efficacy, tolerance, mode of administration, dosage regimen, duration of treatment, price, etc.) with the objective to be delivered at affordable price. Their goal is first to support clinical research (Phase 2 and Phase 3 clinical trials) and then to facilitate the access of treatment for the greatest number of people, especially the most vulnerable populations.

> The mission of DNDi is to develop safe, effective and affordable new treatments for patients suffering from neglected diseases, and to ensure equitable access to these treatments.

Primarily located in low-income countries, platform partners vary according to the goals pursued. They generally include national disease control programmes where they exist, health ministries, universities, civil society representatives, pharmaceutical companies, health professionals, patients' associations, and are open to donors. Currently, DNDi has three active platforms: the Chagas Clinical Research Platform created in Brazil in 2009 (400 members; 22 countries; 100 institutions); the Human African Trypanosomiasis Platform created in 2005 in the Democratic Republic of the Congo (120 members; eight countries; 20 institutions); and the Leishmaniasis East Africa Platform created in 2003 in Sudan (60 members; four countries; 13 institutions).[11]

One must note that, while initiated and funded by DNDi, these platforms do not belong to DNDi but to the medical and scientific community that works within them. Their fundamental objective is to consolidate new skills and introduce them into national and local programmes, thereby strengthening local infrastructure.

DNDi's Innovative Intellectual Property Rights Policy

In the field of Intellectual Property Rights Policy, DNDi's distinction lies in the fact that its policy relies first and foremost on the primacy of access to treatment, as set by its founding documents which state that "the mission of DNDi is to develop safe, effective and affordable new treatments for patients suffering from neglected diseases, and to ensure equitable access to these treatments". This commitment to initiate affordable treatments for which access is equitable has given rise to an innovative IP policy designed to make it possible, if necessary, to reconcile the right of access to treatment of underprivileged and poor populations and the right that certain research partners, especially pharmaceutical companies involved in the research process, can retain to exploit under given limits the molecules shared in the platforms on which they hold patents.

In this way, DNDi is fully committed to a concept of ownership seen as a bundle of rights, a characteristic of the commons approach, whereby different attributes of property rights are distributed and allocated to different types of partners.[12]

Multiple Forms of the Bundles of Rights

A variety of examples with the private sector illustrate the different solutions, implemented and described above. One of them is the partnership concluded in 2008 between DNDi and Anacor, a biotech company since then acquired by Pfizer. This agreement gave DNDi access to a class of therapeutic compounds, held by Anacor, whose applications were still unknown. DNDi could conduct research for a specific indication, sleeping sickness. DNDi was granted non-exclusive rights to the molecule(s) for all applications that may result from its research in this field, while Anacor retained their rights for any other indication. Other examples include the development of the antimalarial ASAQ Winthrop by DNDi and Sanofi, the licensed agreement between DNDi and Presidio Pharmaceuticals on treatment for hepatitis C, or the agreements signed with Abbvie and Sanofi.[5]

Thus, IP policy is designed, through appropriate allocation of rights to the different partners to safeguard the principle of "needs driven" R&D activity and the benefits and access to treatment to a large number of people, especially the most vulnerable populations.[13]

The Shift from "Neglected Diseases" to "Neglected Patients": Challenges and opportunities

In 2015 DNDi decided to take an additional step when DNDi's mission evolved from "neglected diseases" to encompass "neglected patients". This shift represented a major change. Indeed, the broadening of DNDi's focus called for some modifications of its business model. One of the challenges was to gather additional revenue to be able to face this new expanded mission. How can DNDi evolve and scale-up and remain truthful to this mission? More specifically, the question that appeared was: can DNDi effectively derive additional resources from IP – since it is basically an entity dedicated to R&D activities – while keeping true to its founding principles?

Whilst this is largely hypothetical, some options are worth mentioning in order to open up future discussions.

Differentiated Pricing Based on License Policy

One source of additional revenue could be generated from the transfer of licences and hence of exploitation rights at prices that vary according to populations and/or territories. It somewhat interestingly evokes the commons-based 'reciprocity licences' used in many fields, especially open-source software. According to this practice, the commoners who have invested time and resources in the production of the shared material have free and unimpeded access to the licenced material produced by the commons. On the other hand, third parties who have not participated in such production may use the material in exchange for the payment of a compensation to the commons. Reciprocity licensing is an avenue worth exploring to safeguard the principle of needs-driven research. These licenses may represent an opportunity by *reducing the burden for fundraising (and the competition with other NGOs for these funds) while increasing the organisation's autonomy to pursue its own objectives.*

Funding for Dual Destination Drugs

DNDi's shift from neglected diseases to neglected people could lead to investments in diseases and drugs that target patients, not only in developing but also in developed countries. For instance, DNDi is developing a new hepatitis treatment potentially addressing markets in developed countries. DNDi could therefore become eligible for grants and/or contracts with different research organisations. DNDi's ability to develop molecules and bring them to the market at costs considerably lower than those dictated by pharmaceutical companies held to huge payments to satisfy their shareholders, could generate significant savings for these countries. DNDi could therefore receive funds in the form of grants or advances for its commitment to research projects of national interest. In return, the research results and hence the compounds would be governed by special licenses allowing their use for free or at greatly reduced prices, once they are included on the lists of prescribed drugs reimbursed by social healthcare systems.

To conclude, we would argue that since pursuing its primary mission – the promotion of access to safe, effective and affordable treatments to the neediest – DNDi has succeeded in transforming public health into a common good, at least in the field of neglected diseases. Thus, DNDi already constitutes a distinctive illustration of the commons approach in the area of public health.

More generally we can observe that the commons approach is not only insightful today: it also sheds light on the importance of the changes to come for DNDi, in the context of a shift from neglected diseases to neglected people. All commons, including DNDi, cannot live off donations and grants indefinitely. Their sustainability depends on their ability to continue to diversify their funding sources and to generate their own resources more substantially. The capability of commons to create institutions and business models that satisfy essential needs while guaranteeing universal access, especially for the neediest, is without doubt essential for the future of our societies.

This paper is based on the following working paper: "DNDi, a Distinctive Illustration of Commons in the Area of Public Health", Abecassis et al. (2019), AFD Research Papers #2019-93

16. ON THE COMMONS AND EUROPE

Michel Bauwens, Silke Helfrich
and David Bollier

On the Commons and Europe

with Michel Bauwens, Silke Helfrich and David Bollier

Michel Bauwens, Silke Helfrich and David Bollier are three of the most reknowned commons-thinkers in the world. Michel Bauwens is the co-founder of the P2P Foundation, one of the most important organisations in the commons movement. He is the author of countless important publications about the commons. Together with Vasilis Kostakis and Alex Pazaitis, he just released a new book titled Peer To Peer: The Commons Manifesto (2019).[1] Silke Helfrich and David Bollier co-founded the Commons Strategies Group with Michel Bauwens. Helfrich and Bollier also co-wrote two important works about the commons in recent years: The Wealth of the Commons (2012) and Patterns of Commoning (2015). In September of 2019, the duo will release their latest book: Free, Fair and Alive: The Insurgent Power of the Commons (2019), a truly seminal work for anyone interested in the commons.[2] David Bollier is also a board member of Commons Network.

Thomas de Groot: Out of all the major crises we face today, which one is the most urgent?

Silke Helfrich: You mean: Which are the most important factors that led to the interconnected crises we are facing?

David Bollier: Good point, because from the perspective of the commons, the question is self-contradictory. The power of commoning is precisely that authority and action are distributed. Diverse players in particular local settings can determine their own fates, using rules that make sense for them in their special contexts. So even theoretically there is no 'single, most urgent struggle'. There are always multiple arenas of meaningful struggle and one can never know in advance which one will shock and surprise everyone with impressive results. This is also known as resilience.

Michel Bauwens: David is right. Nonetheless, the most urgent question today is undoubtedly climate change, which is itself an expression of deeper structural problems that we must tackle at the same time as a context for solving climate disruption.

> We are immersed in an epistemological delirium – as Bruno Latour would put it. When we think of nature as a resource to be used for our purposes, we imply that it is separated from us!

TdG: What are these deeper structural or systemic problems?

MB: In my analysis, the structural problem is threefold. First of all, we believe that nature and natural resources, that we unfortunately see as being 'outside' ourselves, are infinite resources to be used for human need and private profit. Second, we believe that resources that are eminently shareable, and should be shared to advance humankind, should be made artificially scarce, so we privatize and marketize knowledge, making it unavailable for advancing the common good and solving issues more quickly. Finally, we develop our societies in ways that create inequality and increasing social instability, leading to more and more authoritarian outcomes.

SH: I'd like to highlight one of the aspects Michel points to. The deeper problem is the way we think; or more precisely, the way we are taught to think. We are immersed in an epistemological delirium – as Bruno Latour would put it. An example: when we think of nature as a resource to be used for our purposes, we imply that it is separated from us! Framed that way, everything comes down to a management problem – the management of something. And then we manage and manage and at the end of the day, we get burned out, suffering from that cultivated separation. So, the root cause of the problems mentioned by Michel, and of many other problems, is that we ignore the most important element that makes us truly thrive: relatedness, connection.

DB: Exactly. Any of us could prioritize certain problems, but the more critical challenge is identifying the most suitable framework for understanding them. Climate change and inequality are obvious mega-problems, but what really matters is adopting the correct ontological premises and epistemology. This is so important because we need to frame our problems right – identify their most important dimensions -- if we want to address them effectively.

SH: Right, this means that we need to go a level deeper and look at the way we conceive the world and conceive ourselves as human beings. If these conceptions are too limited or shallow, or if they presume that human beings are merely hyper-rational, utility-maximizing machines the way economics does, the "solutions" that follow will be based on an erroneous foundation.

DB: True. In our new book, Free Fair and Alive, we call this 'the OntoSeed'. If the seed we plant is 'flawed', the yield will be disappointing – or worse, doomed to fail.

SH: It's like the DNA that contains a certain programme that unfolds and we have only a certain impact on the results it brings about. If it is structurally flawed, there is almost nothing we can do about it.

Mutualization of physical resources and provisioning systems has an enormous capacity to diminish the human footprint while maintaining complex social systems for human wellbeing.

In their book[2] Free, Fair and Alive, Bollier and Helfrich write: "Enacting Peer Governance needs to be a living, developmental process in itself. Therefore, instead of offering a full set of prescriptive formulas, our patterns amount to procedural guidelines that enable a stepwise, adaptable path for developing a commons. Enacting a commons through Peer Governance resembles the way in which DNA provides general guidance, but not strict instructions, for the autonomous development and differentiation of an embryo. "Does the DNA contain a full description of the organism to which it will give rise?" asks British biologist Lewis Wolpert. "The answer is no. The genome contains instead a program of instructions for making the organism — a generative program ..." So, the bad news is that there is no blueprint, no panacea. Peer Governance is not a prescriptive, rule-driven program for fabricating commons or managing resources. But the good news is that Peer Governance is a generative process. It is a reliable means by which commoners can build authentic, living relationships among themselves, and in so doing, develop a coherent, stable commons." [TdG]

DB: Indeed. The 'OntoSeed', in turn, affects the structural analyses that are possible and how we can respond. Conventional market-based solutions, international treaties, and state regulation -- for example -- are not going to overcome deep, systemic problems because they are based on the same premises that gave rise to the problems in the first place. They presume homo economicus as an idealized model of a human being, which has proven itself incapable of responding to both scientific evidence and urgent collective-action needs.

SH: And this homo economicus is conceived as an isolated being that focuses on self-maximizing its individual gain. The problem is, that by believing in this story and shaping our institutions accordingly, we actually become a homo economicus. But this conception of ourselves as human beings will not ever make us realise our full potential.

Knowledge, code and design can simply be shared widely and generously, because they become more useful for everybody as we share them. The only thing that prevents us from sharing knowledge generously is the socio-economic model that surrounds us, aka capitalism.

TdG: What do the commons have to offer in response?

MB: We have made substantial progress in recreating commons of shared knowledge, and have started redistribution mechanisms, like urban commons, using commons-centric ecosystems, but it is vital to move the commons-centric economic and social systems to actual material production, as is now already happening in food and energy. Why is this vital: First of all because mutualization and pooling of knowledge, makes sure that all innovations and solutions can be replicated, learned from, and adapted, wherever they are needed. Next, because mutualization of physical resources and provisioning systems has an enormous capacity to diminish the human footprint while maintaining complex social systems for human wellbeing. And finally, because the commons-based model of cosmo-local production[3], whereby 'all that is light is global and shared and all that is heavy is localized to the extent possible', is also one that can regenerate local and bioregional economies, where we can move from extractive economic models, to generative economic models, that heal the earth, its resources and communities. Transforming our means of production and distribution will be vital, by integrating all positive and negative, social and ecological externalities, at all levels of human decision-making.

SH: I agree in general, but I think that we have to pay a lot of attention to the way we conceptualize things. An example: the idea of "mutualizing knowledge" does not make sense to me, at least not in a commons context. Knowledge, code and design can simply be shared widely and generously, because they become more useful for everybody as we share them. The only thing that prevents us from sharing knowledge generously is the socio-economic model that surrounds us, aka capitalism. It is only in this context that it is functional to make what is abundant – such as knowledge – artificially scarce. The purpose for doing this, of course, is to ensure that potential competitors are kept at distance and that everything can be traded on the market. Markets require scarcity in order to work!

Furthermore, we need to be very careful, almost meticulous, not only with the concepts we refer to, but with our wording. We can hardly be truly transformative if we use the language of market economics, state power, and political liberalism. I actually think that we need to come up with a language that is able to capture the essence of commoning and its transformative power. Rather than isolated I's and homo economicus, we are "Nested I's!" – biological and social creatures with deep relational connections and dependencies.

> By asserting a coherent alternative vision, the commons as a discourse begins the process of changing politics and culture. It opens up a space for talking about practical alternatives that escape the destructive logic of neoliberal capitalism and state power as historically exercised.

DB: The great potential of the commons lies in helping us re-imagine what human beings actually are -- and then to re-orient our perspectives, policies, laws, and institutions accordingly. The commons is at one level a discourse and political history, but more fundamentally it is a set of social practices and ethical values that honor fairness, self-determination, inclusion, and responsibility aligned with entitlements. The commons is pre-political in the sense that commoning is an ancient impulse of humanity. It tends to precede any political system and function somewhat autonomously.

The commons points to a different vision of how society might be ordered, relative to modernity and capitalism. It emphasizes peer governance and provisioning at a more local, participatory level. It prioritizes fairness and inclusion. It is not about maximum material throughput -- growth, consumerism, profit, GDP -- but about responsible long-term stewardship on behalf of all. By asserting a coherent alternative vision, the commons as a discourse begins the process of changing politics and culture. It opens up a space for talking about practical alternatives that escape the destructive logic of neoliberal capitalism and state power as historically exercised.

TdG: What is the role of institutions?

MB: The role of institutions, and thus of European institutions, must change their focus from their functioning as market-centric state forms, and the EU certainly has very strong neoliberal biases which block many necessary pathways, towards commons-centric public-social partnerships.

SH: Which we could call Commons/Public Partnerships, commons first, of course.

MB: Yes. And territorial common good institutions can eliminate the multitude of obstacles standing in the way of collaboration and mutualization, and facilitate the autonomy of civil society actors at the personal and collective level.

DB: As commons grow in size and influence, some sort of *modus vivendi* is needed between the state (law, bureaucracy, policy, representative law-making) and the very different logic and ethic of commoning, which is more ecologically and socially grounded. The state may have legality on its side, but the commons more often has social and moral legitimacy.

> Instead of presuming that markets are the only efficient way to produce wealth (when in fact, they are often merely extractive and predatory for private gain), policymakers need to recognize that commons are value-generating social systems.

TdG: What can commoners do to change these institutions?

MB: Beyond public-commons cooperation protocols and mechanisms, there is also a necessary process of the commonification of public services, so that the public resources become inalienable and governed 'poly-centrically' by the multiple stakeholders.

SH: Yeah, we need to -- metaphorically speaking -- put up stickers everywhere and shout out: "This is not for sale, because it is ours." But we also need to get clarity about who is "us" and what rights and obligations this process of commonification entails. After all, we should not forget that commons comes from Latin cum + munus. Cum (English "with") denotes the joining of elements. Munus — which is also found in the word "municipality" — means service, duty, obligation, and sometimes gift. All terms that conjoin cum and munus, such as communion, community, communism, and, of course, communication, point to a co-obligation — or a linkage between use rights, benefits, and duty.

MB: This means that poly-centric governance includes a special role for all citizens but also specifically for transition agents which can prove their impacts. We must overcome the merely competitive public procurement processes and mobilize the whole society towards the eco-social transition. Contributory democracy means that multi-governed institutions can give a place at the decision-making table to commons-oriented civic communities that are exemplars for the transition. Collective institutions like the EU must become commons-facilitating institutions, that start judging projects and initiatives on their regenerative, common good impact, and are thereby able to promote and finance regenerative activity, by mobilizing the whole society and not just firms, and by creating a planning framework of global thresholds and allocations, which can be used granularly at every level, so that production of human needs (and all other beings) can proceed within planetary boundaries and resource boundaries. The role of territorial organizations like the EU is to focus also on capacity building, so that commons engagement can be undertaken by all citizens at their full capacity. One of their central tasks is to help strengthen 'commons of capabilities'.

DB: But how can state power and commoning coexist? That is a significant challenge that commoners and European policymakers alike must address. A first priority should be to decriminalize commoning in cases where it is illegal, such as in seed-sharing and certain forms of information-sharing. We also need new types of law to affirmatively support commoning. It has taken ingenious "legal hacks" such as Creative Commons licenses, the General Public License for free software, and community land trusts to make certain forms of sharing explicitly legal and practical. Instead of presuming that markets are the only efficient way to produce wealth (when in fact, they are often merely extractive and predatory for private gain), policymakers need to recognize that commons are value-generating social systems. Even better, the commons usually do so without the "externalities" that businesses routinely impose upon the environment, communities, and future generations.

TdG: What would a transition of these roles and mentalities of institutions look like?

MB: Climate change, the vital necessary transition towards a mode of production and distribution that is fully compatible with the maintenance of life, the health of the planet, is certainly the fight of our times, but it cannot succeed without more social equity and massive sharing of knowledge. Which means that it becomes a vast process of eco-social transition processes, not just focused on mere decarbonisation. One of the associated priorities is to create means of managing human production that fully integrate externalties, and therefore, the accounting and management of externalities is also a vital part of the transition. Humans must become thermo-dynamically informed in their productive decision-making and society as a whole must become life-centric, not only for humans but for all life and beings, and future generations. This goes well beyond mitigation towards generative and regenerative models. None of this can succeed without giving commons, a vastly more important place in the way society and its institutions are organized. The common good, and nature, must have a voice, and we need institutions that allow for this voice to be heard, not occassionally but as the vast ground of all human decisions.

DB: An added benefit of a commons-based strategy is greater resilience and popular empowerment by distributing authority more widely and at appropriate levels (the idea of "subsidiarity"), rather than concentrating too much power with politicians and centralized bureaucracies. By deconcentrating power, state assistance to commons would in effect promote greater democratic participation and control while reducing large-scale abuses of power and ecological harm.

> The common good, and nature, must have a voice, and we need institutions that allow for this voice to be heard, not occassionally but as the vast ground of all human decisions.

TdG: Can you give me some examples of practices that have inspired you recently?

DB: Commons/public partnerships in which the state actively and in good faith assists the work of commons, have already been mentioned. Imagine expanding the Drugs for Neglected Diseases Initiative, DNDi, which is a partnership among commons, state institutions, and private companies to reduce the costs of drug R&D and distribution. DNDi releases medically important drugs under royalty-free, non-exclusive licenses so that benefits so that the drugs can be made available everywhere inexpensively.

Or consider how the Humanitarian OpenStreetMap Team has helped various states in the wake of natural disasters, such as the earthquake in Haiti. HOT is a commons-driven solution that brings together volunteer hackers to produce invaluable web maps showing first-responders and victims where to find hospitals, water, and other necessities.

The System of Rice Intensification is a global open-source community that trades advice and knowledge about the agronomy of growing rice. Working totally outside of conventional multilateral channels, SRI has brought together farmers in Sri Lanka and Cuba, India and Indonesia, to improve their rice yields by two or three-fold.

The state could help decommodify land and make it more available to ordinary people through community land trusts. If this is the agenda, special attention should be paid to developing commons-friendly infrastructure. This could be hugely beneficial, as seen in community-owned Wi-Fi like Guifi.net, free and open source software, and regional food systems that empower smaller farmers and enterprises.

Developing legal hacks that can provide legal recognition to commoning is vital. Platform cooperatives that offer alternatives to the "gig economy" (Uber) are one innovation that needs support. So are certain distributed ledger technologies such as Holochain, which aims to be a commons-friendly alternative to the blockchain as emboded in Bitcoin.

Ultimately, the most urgent struggle is not to "pick battles to fight" with the state or ideological adversaries, or to attempt to seize state power, an achievement that may be Pyrrhic, as the experience of Syriza has shown. The most urgent struggle is to build out the world of commoning as a parallel social economy with its own stability, autonomy, and effectiveness. That is the foundational base upon which a transformational politics can be built.

SH: Exactly. State institutions are misconstrued as solutions when they are often part of the problem. Representative democracy purports to be fair and effective, but because it is hierarchical and corrupted by money – the wider problem of 'Governing-through-Money' – it is not TRULY representative and centralized bureaucracies have trouble being responsive to dynamic, local circumstances. I think we have to ask ourselves if commons and commoning can be reconciled with representative democracy and bureaucracy, and if so, how. The challenge for all of us is to learn to think like a commoner and to feel like a commoner. This basically means to learn to really feel and recognize that we are inescapably related to each other – to see that we are interdependent on each other and that my personal development depends on the development of yours, and vice versa.

References and Resources

Introduction: Shifting Paradigms

1. Habermas, J. *Die Einbeziehung des Anderen - Studien zur politischen Theorie* (Suhrkamp, 1996). https://www.suhrkamp.de/buecher/die_einbeziehung_des_anderen-juergen_habermas_29044.html

The Potential of the Commons, with Kate Raworth and George Monbiot

1. Raworth, K. (2017) *Doughnut Economics: Seven Ways to Think Like a 21st-Century Economist* (Random House Business, 2017) https://www.penguin.co.uk/books/110/1107761/doughnut-economics/9781847941398.html

2. Monbiot, G. (2017) *Out of the Wreckage: A New Politics in the Age of Crisis* (Verso, 2017) https://www.versobooks.com/books/2732-out-of-the-wreckage

3. Hardin, G. (1968) *The Tragedy of the Commons*. Science, 162: 1243. https://science.sciencemag.org/content/162/3859/1243

4. 'Partner State', see for instance: http://wiki.p2pfoundation.net/Partner_State

5. 'Mission-oriented innovation policy' by Mariana Mazzucato, see for instance: https://marianamazzucato.com/research/green-innovation/

Commons-based Renewable Energy in the Age of Climate Collapse, by David Hammerstein

1. Diamond, J. Collapse: *How Societies Choose to Fail or Survive* (Penguin, 2011). https://www.penguin.co.uk/books/24872/collapse/9780241958681.html

2. *Global Resources Outlook 2019*, UN International Resource Panel. http://www.resourcepanel.org/sites/default/files/documents/document/media/unep_252_global_resource_outlook_2019_web.pdf

3. 'Green New Deal'?, qué 'Green New Deal'?, Luis Gonzáles Reyes, CTXT Magazine, April 3rd, 2019: https://ctxt.es/es/20190403/Firmas/25368/green-new-deal-transicion-ecologica-smart-cities-luis-gonzalez-reyes.htm

4. *World Energy Investment 2018*, report, International Energy Agency. https://

www.iea.org/wei2018/

5. Renewables 2018 Global Status Report, Renewable Energy Policy Netork for the 21st Century. http://www.ren21.net/wp-content/uploads/2018/06/17-8652_GSR2018_FullReport_web_final_.pdf

6. Polimeni, J. M., Kozo, M., Giampietro, M., Alcott, B. *The Jevons Paradox and the myth of resource efficiency improvements* (Earthscan, 2008)

7. Raworth, K. *Doughnut Economics: Seven Ways to Think Like a 21st-Century Economist* (Random House Business, 2017) https://www.penguin.co.uk/books/110/1107761/doughnut-economics/9781847941398.html

8. Wolsink, M., Hevelpund, F. et al. *Local Communities and Social Innovation for the Energy Transition*, Workshop Booklet, Joint Research Centre of the European Commission. 2018 https://www.researchgate.net/profile/Maarten_Wolsink/publication/329813977_Local_Communities_and_Social_Innovation_for_the_Energy_Transition_Workshop_Booklet_Event_Organised_by_the_European_Commission-Joint_Research_Centre/links/5c1bddb8299bf12be38ee546/Local-Communities-and-Social-Innovation-for-the-Energy-Transition-Workshop-Booklet-Event-Organised-by-the-European-Commission-Joint-Research-Centre.pdf

9. Community Energy Coalition / Energy Cities, *Unleashing the Power of Community Renewable Energy*, 2019 http://www.energy-cities.eu/IMG/pdf/community_energy_booklet_2018_en.pdf

10. Hickel, J., Kallis, G. (2019) *Is Green Growth Possible?*, New Political Economy, April 2019 https://www.tandfonline.com/doi/full/10.1080/13563467.2019.1598964

Energy Commons: The Missing Link Between Energy Transition and Climate Justice, by Cecile Blanchet

1. Rescoop, homepage, accessed on May 8th 2019, https://www.rescoop.eu/

2. Energy Transition, homepage, accessed on May 8th 2019, https://energytransition.org/

3. DGRV (the German Association for Cooperatives) 2017 Year Report, *Energiegenossenschaften* 2017, https://www.genossenschaften.de/sites/default/files/Umfrage_Energiegenossenschaften_2018_DGRV.pdf

4. *Power to the people: Upholding the right to clean, affordable energy for all in the EU*, Research Report from the Right to Energy coalition, February 2019.

https://righttoenergy.files.wordpress.com/2019/02/ep-report-18.02.19.pdf

5. *Fuel Poverty Action Plan*, policy plan by the London Municipal Government, June 2018. https://www.london.gov.uk/WHAT-WE-DO/environment/environment-publications/fuel-poverty-action-plan

6. *Reclaiming Public Services: How Cities and Citizens Are Turning Back Privatisation*, Research Report by TNI (Transnational Institute), June 2017. https://www.tni.org/files/publication-downloads/reclaiming_public_services.pdf

7. *The German Energy Transition*, press fact sheet by the Berlin Energy Transition Dialogue, March 2016. https://www.energiewende2018.com/wp-content/uploads/2016/03/BETD2016_Press_Factsheet_Layout_1603.pdf

8. Green Grant Delaware homepage, accessed May 8th 2019, http://greengrantdelaware.com/

9. Byrne, J., Martinez, C., Ruggero, C. (2009) *Relocating Energy in the Social Commons: Ideas for a Sustainable Energy Utility*, Bulletin of Science, Technology & Society, 29:2; 81-94. https://cpb-us-w2.wpmucdn.com/sites.udel.edu/dist/3/848/files/2013/08/2009_pe_BSTS_relocating_emergy_social_commons_Byrne_Martinez_Ruggero_3.pdf

10. *Democratising Energy Course 01: Energy Colonialism, Energy*, Commons and the Rest, November 2016. https://energycommonsblog.wordpress.com/2016/11/05/democratising-energy-course-01-energy-colonialism/

Territories of Commons in Europe: Niches of a Much Needed Transition, by Jose Luis Vivero Pol

1. *Towards a Common Food Policy for the EU*, iPES FOOD research report, February 2019: http://www.ipes-food.org/pages/CommonFoodPolicy

2. Vivero-Pol, J. L. (2017) *Food as Commons or Commodity? Exploring the Links between Normative Valuations and Agency in Food Transition*. Sustainability, 9, 442. https://www.mdpi.com/2071-1050/9/3/442

3. Vivero Pol, J. L., Schuftan, C. (2016) *No right to food and nutrition in the SDGs: mistake or success?*. BMJ Global Health, 1, 40. https://gh.bmj.com/content/1/1/e000040

4. Vivero-Pol, J. L., Ferrando, T., De Schutter, O., Mattei, U. *Routledge Handbook of Food as a Commons* (Routledge, 2019) https://www.routledge.com/Routledge-Handbook-of-Food-as-a-Commons/Vivero-Pol-Ferrando-

Schutter-Mattei/p/book/9781138062627

5. *The Food Commons in Europe*, **Jose Luis Vivero-Pol, P2P Foundation Blog, February 1st 2017:** https://blog.p2pfoundation.net/food-commons-europe/2017/02/01

6. *Territories of Commons in Europe*, **Jose Luis Vivero-Pol, P2P Foundation Wiki, November 2016:** http://wiki.p2pfoundation.net/Territories_of_Commons_in_Europe

7. *États Capturés: Les Gouvernements Nationaux, Défenseurs des Intérets Privés au Sein de l'EU*, **Corporate Europe Observatory, February 2019:** https://corporateeurope.org/sites/default/files/captured-states-exec-summary-fr.pdf

8. Curtis, D. R. (2016) *Did the Commons Make Medieval and Early Modern Rural Societies More Equitable? A Survey of Evidence from across Western Europe*, **1300–1800. Journal of Agrarian Change, 16: 646– 664.** https://onlinelibrary.wiley.com/action/showCitFormats?doi=10.1111%2Fjoac.12101

9. Axelby, R. (2007) *'It Takes Two Hands to Clap': How Gaddi Shepherds in the Indian Himalayas Negotiate Access to Grazing*. **Journal of Agrarian Change, 7: 35-75.** https://onlinelibrary.wiley.com/doi/10.1111/j.1471-0366.2007.00139.x

10. *Commons and 'Commoning': A 'New' Old Narrative to Enrich the Food Sovereignty and Right to Food Claims*, **Tomaso Ferrando, Jose Luis Vivero-Pol, Right To Food And Nutrition, September 26th, 2017:** https://www.righttofoodandnutrition.org/commons-and-commoning-new-old-narrative-enrich-food-sovereignty-and-right-food-claims

Social Circularity: Food-sharing Platforms Are Re-inventing Urban Solidarity, by Thomas de Groot

1. **FoodTopia homepage, accessed on May 3rd, 2019:** http://foodtopia.eu/

2. **BuurtBuik homepage, accessed on May 3rd, 2019:** https://buurtbuik.nl/

3. *Bruto Binnenlands Product*, **CBS (Dutch Bureau of Statistics), accessed on May 3rd, 2019:** https://www.cbs.nl/nl-nl/onze-diensten/in-de-klas/conjunctuurbekerstrijd/te-voorspellen-indicatoren/bruto-binnenlands-product--bbp--

4. *Meer Huishoudens Met Risico Op Armoede in 2017*, **CBS (Dutch Bureau of Statistics), November 12th, 2018:** https://www.cbs.nl/nl-nl/nieuws/2018/46/meer-huishoudens-met-risico-op-armoede-in-2017

5. *Kerncijfers Armoede In Amsterdam*, **OIS (Amsterdam Bureau of Statistics),
July 16th, 2018:** https://www.ois.amsterdam.nl/nieuws/kerncijfers-armoede-in-amsterdam

6. *Eenzaamheid, Cijfers en Context*, **Volksgezondheid en Zorg (Information
portal of Dutch Ministry of Health), accessed on May 3rd, 2019:** https://
www.volksgezondheidenzorg.info/onderwerp/eenzaamheid/cijfers-context/
samenvatting

7. *Eenzaamheid in Amsterdam*, **OIS (Amsterdam Bureau of Statistics), March
12th, 2018:** https://www.ois.amsterdam.nl/nieuwsarchief/2018/eenzaamheid-in-amsterdam

8. *Veel Mensen Die In Armoede Verkeren*, **Voelen Zich Sterk Eenzaam,
Samen Tegen Eenzaamheid, October 18th, 2017:** https://www.
samentegeneenzaamheid.nl/blog/risicogroepen/veel-mensen-die-armoede-verkeren-voelen-zich-sterk-eenzaam

9. *Armoede En Uitsluiting*, **CBS (Dutch Bureau of Statistics), December 16th,
2015:** https://www.cbs.nl/nl-nl/publicatie/2015/51/armoede-en-sociale-uitsluiting-2015

10. *Fact Check: 'Amsterdammers Gooien Eten Weg Voor 60.000 Mensen'*, **NRC,
July 12th, 2014:** https://www.nrc.nl/nieuws/2014/07/12/amsterdammers-gooien-eten-weg-voor-60000-mensen-1399980-a198339

11. *Food Wastage Footprint and Climate Change*, **report, UN Food and
Agriculture Organization, accessed on May 3rd, 2019:** http://www.fao.org/
nr/sustainability/food-loss-and-waste

12. *The Climate Impact of the Food in the Back of Your Fridge*, **Chad Frischmann,
The Washington Post, July 31st, 2018:** https://www.washingtonpost.com/
news/theworldpost/wp/2018/07/31/food-waste/

Ostrom in the City: Design Principles and Practices for the Urban Commons, by Christian Iaione and Sheila Foster

1. Sassen, S. (2015) *Expulsions: Brutality and complexity in the global economy*
(Belknap/Harvard, 2015)

2. Foster, S. R. (2006) *The City as an Ecological Space: Social Capital and Urban
Land Use.* **Notre Dame Law Review 82: 527**

3. Ostrom, E. (1990) *Governing the Commons: The Evolution of Institutions for
Collective Action* **(Cambridge University Press, 1990)**

4. Jacobs, J. (1961) *The Death and Life of Great American Cities* (Random House, 1961)

5. Rae, D. (2003) *City: Urbanism at its End* (Yale University Press, 2003)

6. Linebaugh, P. (2008) *The Magna Carta Manifesto: Liberties and Commons for All*, (University of California Press, 2008) https://provisionaluniversity.files.wordpress.com/2012/12/peter-linebaugh-the-magna-carta-manifesto-liberties-and-commons-for-all-2008.pdf

7. Foster, S.R. and Iaione, C. (2016) *The City as a Commons*, Yale Law and Policy Review 34: 281

8. Ostrom, V., Tiebout, C.M. & Warren, R. (1961) *The Organization of Government in Metropolitan Areas: A Theoretical Inquiry*, American Political Science Review, 55, pp. 831-42.

9. Ostrom, E. (2010b) *Polycentric Systems for Coping with Collective Action and Global Environmental Change*, Global Environmental Change 20: 550-557

10. Ostrom, E. (2005) *Unlocking Public Entrepreneurship and Public Economies*, Working Paper DP2005/01, World Institute for Development Economic Research (UNU-WIDER) https://www.wider.unu.edu/publication/unlocking-public-entrepreneurship-and-public-economies

11. Foster, S.R. (2011) *Collective Action and the Urban Commons*, Notre Dame Law Review 87: 57

12. Iaione, C. (2010) *The Tragedy of Urban Roads: Saving Cities from Choking, Calling on Citizens to Combat Climate Change*, Fordham Urbam Law Journal 37:3 https://ir.lawnet.fordham.edu/ulj/vol37/iss3/7/

13. Iaione C. (2015), *Governing the Urban Commons*, Italian Journal of Public Law, 2015, 170

14. Co-Cities homepage, accessed on May 8th 2019. http://commoning.city/

15. Fennell, L.A. (2015) *Agglomerama*, Brigham Young University Law Review, 2014: 1373-1414

16. Frischmann, B.M. (2012), *Infrastructure - The Social Value of Shared Resources*. Oxford University Press

17. Fennell, L.A. (2004) *Common Interest Tragedies*, Northwestern Law Review, 98: 907-990

18. Ostrom, E. (2010a) *Beyond markets and states: Polycentric governance of complex economic systems*, American Economic Review 100: 641-72

19. Madison, Michael J., Brett M. Frischmann and Katherine J. Strandburg. (2014) *Governing Knowledge Commons*, in Governing Knowledge Commons, Oxford University Press, Oxford

20. Hess, C. (2008) *Mapping the New Commons*, Working Paper, available at: https://ssrn.com/abstract=1356835

21. Unnikrishnan H., Manjunatha, B. & Nagendra, H. (2016) *Contested urban commons: mapping the transition of a lake to a sports stadium in Bangalore.* International Journal of the Commons. 10(1), pp. 265–293

22. Nagendra, H. and E. Ostrom. (2014) *Applying the Social-Ecological System Framework to the Diagnosis of Urban Lake Commons in Bangalore, India.* Ecology and Society 19:67

23. Madison, Michael J., Brett M. Frischmann and Katherine J. Strandburg. (2010) *Constructing Commons in the Cultural Environment*, Cornell Law Review 95:657-710

24. Bollier D. & Helfrich S. (2015) *Patterns of Commoning*, Commons Strategies Group

25. Bresnihan, P. and Byrne, M (2015) *Escape Into the City: Everyday Practices of Commoning and the Production of Urban Space in Dublin*, Antipode 47: 36-54

26. Ela, N. (2016) *Urban Commons as Property Experiment: Mapping Chicago's Farms and Gardens*, Fordham Urban Law Journal 43 247-294

27. Portugali, J., Meyer, H., Stolk, E., Tan, E. (2012), *Complexity Theories of Cities Have Come of Age*, Springer

28. Hudson, B. and Rosenbloom, J. D., 2013. *Uncommon Approaches to Commons Problems: Nested Governance Commons and Climate Change*, Hastings Law Journal 64: 1273-1342

29. Iaione C. and Elena De Nictolis (2017b), *Urban Pooling*, Fordham Urban Law Journal, 665

30. Iaione C. (2016), *The Co-City*, in American Journal of Economics and Sociology, 415

31. Iaione C. & Cannavo P. (2015) *The Collaborative and Polycentric Governance*

of the Urban and Local Commons, 5 Urb. Pamphleteer 5: 29

32. Hudson, B., Rosenbloom, J., Cole, D. eds (2019) *Routledge Handbook of the Study of the Commons* (Routledge) https://www.routledge.com/Routledge-Handbook-of-the-Study-of-the-Commons-1st-Edition/Hudson-Rosenbloom-Cole/p/book/9781138060906

Designing, Sustaining and Defending Resilient Urban Commons: The Story of R-Urban, by Doina Petrescu and Constantin Petcou

1. Negri, A., & Hardt, M. (2009). *Commonwealth*. Cambridge (MA): Harvard University Press.

2. Lewis, M. and Conaty, P. (2012) *The Resilience Imperative: Cooperative Transitions to a Steady-State Economy*. Gabriola Island, Canada: New Society Publishers.

3. Folke, C. et al. (2010) *Resilience thinking: Integrating resilience, adaptability and transformability*. Ecology and Society, 15(4): 20.

4. Ostrom, E. (1990). *Governing the commons: The evolution of institutions for collective action*. New York: Cambridge University Press.

5. Foster, S. and Iaione, C. (2017). Ostrom in the city: Design principles for the urban commons. Retrived at: www.thenatureofcities.com/2017/08/20/ostrom-city-designprinciples-urban-commons/.

6. aaa practice website: www.urbantactics.org ; R-Urban project website: http://r-urban.net

7. R-Urban: http://r-urban.net

8. MacKinnon, D. and Derickson, K.D. (2013) From resilience to resourcefulness: A critique of resilience policy and activism. Progress in Human Geography, 37(2): 253–270.

9. On community economy see Gibson-Graham, K.J., Cameron, J., and Healy, S. (2013) Take Back the Economy: An Ethical Guide for Transforming Our Communities. Minneapolis, MN: University of Minnesota Press.

10. J.K. Gibson-Graham (2011) A feminist project of belonging for the Anthropocene, Gender, Place & Culture: A Journal of Feminist Geography, 18:01, 1-21.

11. Bauwens M. (2015) *Sauver le monde: vers une économie post-capitaliste*

avec le peer-to-peer. **Paris: Les liens qui libèrent**

12. see also Petrescu, D., Petcou, C., and Baibarac, C. (2016) Co-producing commons-based resilience: Lessons from R-Urban. Building Research & Information, 44(7): 717–736.

Could This Local Experiment Be the Start of a National Transformation? by George Monbiot

1. *BNP doubles number of councillors*, **BBC News, May 5th, 2006:** http://news.bbc.co.uk/2/hi/uk_news/politics/4974870.stm

2. *George Monbiot: How Do We Get Out Of This Mess?*, **The Guardian, September 9th, 2017:** https://www.theguardian.com/books/2017/sep/09/george-monbiot-how-de-we-get-out-of-this-mess

3. *What's The Difference Between Bonding and Bridging Social Capital?*, **Social Capital, Research and Training, January 2nd, 2018:** https://www.socialcapitalresearch.com/difference-bonding-bridging-social-capital/

4. **Beyerlein, K., Hipp, J. R.,** *Social Capital, Too Much of a Good Thing? American Religious Traditions and Community Crime*; **Social Forces 84, no. 2 (2005): 995-1013.** http://www.jstor.org/stable/3598488.

5. **Kawashima-Ginsberg, K., Lim, C., Levine, P. (2012)** *Civic Health And Unemployment II: The Case Builds*, **National Conference on Citizenship, 2012.** https://www.academia.edu/11729767/_Civic_Health_and_Unemployment_II_The_Case_Builds

6. **Menahem, G., Doron, G., Itzhak, Haim, D. I (2011)** *Bonding and Bridging Associational Social Capital and the Financial Performance of Local Authorities in Israel*, **Public Management Review, 13:5, 659-681.** https://www.tandfonline.com/doi/abs/10.1080/14719037.2010.532962

7. *BNP Loses All 12 Seats In Barking and Dagenham Council*: **BBC News, May 8th, 2010:** http://news.bbc.co.uk/2/hi/8668885.stm

8. *BNP Thanks Labour Minister For Publicity*, **The Guardian, May 5th, 2006:** https://www.theguardian.com/politics/2006/may/05/localelections2006.uk

9. **Participatory City homepage, accessed on May 3rd, 2019:** http://www.participatorycity.org/

10. *Designed to Scale: Mass Participation To Build Resilient Neighbourhoods*, **Participatory City, August 29th, 2015:** https://issuu.com/participatorycity/

docs/designed_to_scale_v.1

11. *Every One, Every Day*, **London Borough of Barking and Dagenham,** accessed on May 3rd, 2019: https://www.lbbd.gov.uk/every-one-every-day

12. Every One Every Day homepage, accessed on May 3rd, 2019: https://www.weareeveryone.org/

13. Participatory City Year 1 Report: https://drive.google.com/file/d/1Xobnc y0wVby19kjT7li0giGsAtvg8rt3/view

14. Monbiot, George (2019), The Guardian (January 24th, 2019): https://www.theguardian.com/commentisfree/2019/jan/24/neighbourhood-project-barking-dagenham

A New Vision for a Shared Digital Europe, by Alek Tarkowski, Paul Keller and Sophie Bloemen

1. Bloemen, S., Tarkowski, A., Keller, P. (2019), Shared Digital Europe: https://shared-digital.eu

Own This! A Portfolio of Platform Cooperativism in Progress, by Trebor Scholz

B 1. Scholz, T. (2016 a): Platform Cooperativism: Challenging the Corporate Sharing Economy. New York: Rosa Luxemburg Foundation. http://www.rosalux-nyc.org/wp-content/files_mf/scholz_platformcoop_5.9.2016.pdf

2. Scholz, T. (2014). Platform Cooperativism vs. the Sharing Economy. 5. December 2014. https://medium.com/@trebors/platform-cooperativism-vs-the-sharing-economy-2ea737f1b5ad

3. Scholz, T. (2018 a): How to Coop the Digital Economy. Institute of Network Cultures, Amsterdam. http://networkcultures.org/blog/publication/moneylab-reader-2-overcoming-the-hype

4. Scholz, T. (2018 b). The State of Platform Cooperativism at #PDF18. Lecture at Personal Democratic Forum (PDF). 18.June 2018. https://www.youtube.com/watch?v=qcPUARqRsVM

5. Platform Cooperativism Consortium (n.d.). Platform Co-ops: We Connect Cooperatives With The Digital Economy. https://ia601508.us.archive.org/6/items/PLATFORMCOOPERATIVISMGraphicIndividualLetterSizePagesJuly252018/PLATFORM-COOPERATIVISM_graphic-individual-letter-size-pages_%20

July%2025%2C%202018.pdf

6. Scholz, T (2016 b). Uber-Worked and Underpaid: How Workers Are Disrupting the Digital Economy. Cambridge: Polity Press.

7. Anzilotti, E. (2018) Worker-Owned Co-ops Are Coming For The Digital Gig Economy. Fast Company. 31. May 2018. https://www.fastcompany.com/40575728/worker-owned-co-ops-are-coming-for-the-digital-gig-economy

8. Platform Cooperativism (2018). Directory. https://platform.coop/directory

9. Schneider, N. (2016). The Rise of a Cooperatively Owned Internet: Platform Cooperativism Gets a Boost. The Nation. 13. October 2016. https://www.thenation.com/article/the-rise-of-a-cooperatively-owned-internet/

10. Bounds, A. (2018). New Co-operatives Aim to Cut Cost of Student Accommodation. Financial Times. 8. March 2018. https://www.ft.com/content/8c69f682-2b62-11e8-a34a-7e7563b0b0f4

11. Scholz, T./Schneider, N., eds. (2017). Ours to Hack and to Own: Platform Cooperativism. A New Vision for the Future of Work and a Fairer Internet. New York City: OR Books.

Digital Commoning and the Fight for a Human-Centered Internet, by Mai Ishikawa Sutton

1. *UN report singles out homeless conditions in Oakland, San Francisco as 'cruel and inhumane'*, **Fox KTVU, October 25th, 2018:** http://www.ktvu.com/news/un-report-singles-out-homeless-conditions-in-oakland-san-francisco-as-cruel-and-inhumane-

2. *Is your phone tainted by the misery of the 35,000 children in Congo's mines?*, **Siddharth Kara, The Guardian, October 12th, 2018:** https://www.theguardian.com/global-development/2018/oct/12/phone-misery-children-congo-cobalt-mines-drc

3. *Conflict minerals: the bloody truth behind your smartphone*, **European Parliament, News section, March 21st, 2017:** http://www.europarl.europa.eu/news/en/headlines/world/20170314STO66681/conflict-minerals-the-bloody-truth-behind-your-smartphone

4. *Apple's war on repair continues: Amazon now bans refurb Apple products from third parties*, **Cory Doctorow, Boing Boing, November 9th, 2018:** https://boingboing.net/2018/11/09/straight-to-landfill.html

5. *The Über-Lobbyists: how Silicon Valley is changing Brussels lobbying*, **Raphaël Kerguено, Transparency International, May 4th, 2017:** https://transparency.eu/uber-lobbyists/

6. *Airbnb Spends $8 Million Lobbying Against San Francisco Ballot Initiative*, **Huffington Post, January 11th, 2015:** https://www.huffpost.com/entry/airbnb-san-francisco-proposition-f_n_56366676e4b0c66bae5cc3b6

7. *When Uber Left Austin*, **Motherboard/Vice, May 26th, 2016:** https://motherboard.vice.com/en_us/article/yp337g/why-uber-lost-austin

8. *AirBnB lobbies EU to fight cities' attempts to protect affordable housing*, **Corporate Europe Observatory, May 2nd, 2018:** https://corporateeurope.org/en/pressreleases/2018/05/airbnb-lobbies-eu-fight-cities-attempts-protect-affordable-housing

9. *A New Digital Trade Agenda: Good or Bad for Digital Rights?*, **Internet Policy Observatory, accessed on May 3rd, 2019:** http://globalnetpolicy.org/digital-trade-agenda/

10. Tech Workers Coalition homepage, accessed on May 3rd, 2019: https://techworkerscoalition.org/

11. *Meeting Europe's Connectivity Challenge: The Role For Community Networks*, **Internet Society, July 3rd, 2018:** https://www.internetsociety.org/resources/doc/2018/meeting-europes-connectivity-challenge/

12. iFixit homepage, accessed on May 3rd 2019: https://www.ifixit.com/

13. Public Resource homepage, accessed on May 3rd, 2019: https://public.resource.org/index.html

14. *Loomio and the Problem of Deliberation*, **Marco Deseriis, Richard Bartlett, OpenDemocracy, December 2nd, 2016:** https://www.opendemocracy.net/en/digitaliberties/loomio-and-problem-of-deliberation/

From Lab to Commons: Health as a Common Good, by Sophie Bloemen

1. *The People's Prescription: Re-imagining Health Innovation to Deliver Public Value*, **Mariana Mazzucato and others, UCL Institute for Innovation and Public Purpose, IIPP Policy Report, 2018-10:** stopaids.org.uk/wp/wp-content/uploads/2018/10/report.pdf

2. *From Lab to Commons: Shifting to a Public Interest Biomedical System, Sophie*

Bloemen and David Hammerstein, **Commons Network Policy Paper, 2018:** commonsnetwork.org/wp-content/uploads/2018/06/FromLabToCommons. pdf

3. Delinkage, a platform for the delinkage-movement, run by Knowledge Ecology International: [https://delinkage.org/] (http://delinkage.org)

The Medicines Patent Pool: A Remedy for the Anti-Commons, by Ellen 't Hoen

1. *An Essential Health Care Patent Pool*, **powerpoint presentation by James Love, International AIDS Conference 2002:** www.cptech.org/slides/jameslove-barcelona.ppt

2. *The Manufacturer's Aircraft Association*, **fact sheet:** http://www.cptech.org/cm/maa.html

3. *Declaration on the TRIPS Agreement and Public Health*, **World Trade Organisation 'Ministerial', November 2001:** https://www.wto.org/english/thewto_e/minist_e/min01_e/mindecl_trips_e.htm

4. **Commission on Intellectual Property Rights, Innovation and Public Health (CIPIH), World Health Organization, website:** https://www.who.int/intellectualproperty/en/

5. **Heller, M. A., Eisenberg, R., S.** *Can patents deter innovation? the anticommons in biomedical research*. **Science. 1998 May 1;280 (5364):698-701**

6. **Verbeure, B., van Zimmeren, E., Matthijs, G., Van Overwalle, G.** *Patent pools and diagnostic testing*. **Trends in Biotechnology. 2006 March 2006;24 (3):115-120**

7. **Serafino D.** *Survey of patent pools demonstrates variety of purposes and management structures*. **Washington, D.C.: Knowledge Ecology International; 2007 4 June 2007. Report No.: KEI Research Note 2007: 6**

8. *Preliminary Legal Review of Proposed Medicines Patent Pool*, **UNITAID, 2007:** http://www.academia.edu/974517/Preliminary_Legal_Review_of_Proposed_Medicines_Patent_Pool

9. *UNITAID Drug Patent Pool Implementation Hinges On Board, IP-Watch blog*, **Novemebr 12th 2009:** http://www.ip-watch.org/2009/12/11/unitaid-drug-patent-pool-implementation-hinges-on-board

10. *Pharmaceutical Groups Set Up Generics Initiative*, **Financial Times,** https://

www.ft.com/content/5f6e1c54-94fb-11df-af3b-00144feab49a

11. *US National Institutes of Health (NIH) First to Share Patents with Medicines Patent Pool As it Opens for Business*, **press release MPP, September 30th 2010:** https://medicinespatentpool.org/mpp-media-post/us-national-institutes-of-health-nih-first-to-share-patents-with-medicines-patent-pool-as-it-opens-for-business/

12. *US Government First To Share Patents With Medicines Patent Pool*, **from the Obama White House blog, September 30th 2010:** https://obamawhitehouse.archives.gov/blog/2010/09/30/us-government-first-share-patents-with-medicines-patent-pool

13. *Medicines Patent Pool Agreement with Gilead a Key Milestone*, **from the Obama White House blog, July 12th 2011:** https://obamawhitehouse.archives.gov/blog/2011/07/12/medicines-patent-pool-agreement-gilead-key-milestone

14. *Bristol-Myers Squibb and Medicines Patent Pool Increase Access to Critical HIV Drug*, **from the Obama White House blog, December 12th 2013:** https://obamawhitehouse.archives.gov/blog/2013/12/12/bristol-myers-squibb-and-medicines-patent-pool-increase-access-critical-hiv-drug

15. *ViiV Healthcare and the Medicines Patent Pool Expand Access to Latest HIV Drugs*, **from the Obama White House blog, April 4th 2014:** https://obamawhitehouse.archives.gov/blog/2014/04/04/viiv-healthcare-and-medicines-patent-pool-expand-access-latest-hiv-drugs

16. Medicines Patent Pool Announces First Licensing Agreement with a Pharmaceutical Company, press release MPP, July 12th 2011: https://medicinespatentpool.org/mpp-media-post/medicines-patent-pool-announces-first-licensing-agreement-with-a-pharmaceutical-company/

17. *Generic Companies Join the Patent Pool*, **press release MPP, October 11th 2011:** https://medicinespatentpool.org/mpp-media-post/generic-companies-join-the-patent-pool/

18. 't Hoen E. (2016) *Indian hepatitis C drug patent decision shakes public health community*. **The Lancet. 2016 Jun 4;387 (10035):2272-3.** https://www.thelancet.com/journals/lancet/article/PIIS0140-6736(16)30656-0/fulltext

19. *Products Licensed*, **licenses overview on MPP website:** https://medicinespatentpool.org/what-we-do/global-licence-overview/licences-in-the-mpp/

20. *The Medicines Patent Pool Welcomes First Generic Dolutegravir-Combination to Receive Tentative Approval from U.S. Food and Drug Administration*, **MPP press release, August 8th, 2017:** https://medicinespatentpool.org/mpp-media-post/the-medicines-patent-pool-welcomes-first-generic-dolutegravir-combination-to-receive-tentative-approval-from-u-s-food-and-drug-administration/

21. What new GSK patent policy means for the developing world, Nature news blog, April 5th 2016: https://www.nature.com/news/what-new-gsk-patent-policy-means-for-the-developing-world-1.19695

Developing Innovative Drugs Through the Commons, by Benjamin Coriat and co-authors

1. Abecassis P., Coutinet N. (2018) *Économie du médicament, Repères*, **La Découverte 716:127**

2. Malpani R., Heineke C., Kamal-Yann M. (2008) *Mettre fin à la crise de la R&D dans la santé publique*, **information document, Oxfam International, November 2008**

3. Coriat B. (ed.), (2008) *The Political Economy of HIV/AIDS in Developing Countries*. **Edward Elgar, Cheltenham**

4. Coriat B., Orsi F., d'Alameida C. (2006) *TRIPS and the International Public Health Controversies: Issues and Challenges*, **Industrial and Corporate Change, 15:1033–62**

5. Branciard A., (2012) *Des modèles de recherche-développement ouverts et collaboratifs dans le domaine pharmaceutique: vers des « communs » ? DNDi et les enseignements de son antipaludéen* **ASAQ, WP PROPICE 2012-17**

6. Kaul I., Grunberg I. and Stern M. A. (eds) (1999), *Global Public Goods: International Cooperation in the 21st Century*, **Oxford University Press, 1999**

7. Leyronas S. (2018) *Repenser l'Aide publique au développement au prisme des communs;* **in Alix et al. (eds), Le Nouvel Age des Communs. Vers uns République des Biens Communs, Les Liens qui Libèrent, 2018**

8. Boidin B., Hiez D., Rousseau S. (2008) *Biens communs, biens publics mondiaux et propriété*, **Développement durable et territoires, Dossier 10: Joint property and ownership**

9. Coriat (ed) (2015) *Le retour des Communs: La crise de l'idéologie Propriétaire*. **Les Liens qui Libèrent, 2015**

10. Ostrom E. (1990) *Governing the Commons – The Evolution of Institutions for Collective Action.* **New York: Cambridge University Press**

11. DNDi annual report 2017. https://www.dndi.org/annualreport2017/

12. Orsi F. (2015) *Revisiter la propriété pour construire les communs*, **in Coriat (ed) (2015)** *Le retour des Communs: La crise de l'idéologie Propriétaire,* **Les Liens qui Libèrent, Paris**

13. Pecoul, B. (2016) D*rugs for Neglected Diseases Initiative contribution to High-Level Panel on Access to Medicines,* http://www.unsgaccessmeds.org/inbox/2016/2/27/bernard-pecoul

On the Commons and Europe, with Michel Bauwens, Silke Helfrich and David Bollier

1. Bauwens, M., Kostakis, V., Pazaitis, A. (2019). *Peer To Peer: The Commons Manifesto.* **University of Westminster Press.** https://www.uwestminsterpress.co.uk/site/books/10.16997/book33/

2. Bollier, D., Helfrich, S. (2019). *Free, Fair and Alive: The Insurgent Power of the Commons.* **New Society Publishers.** https://www.newsociety.com/Books/F/Free-Fair-and-Alive

3. Ramos, J. (2016). *Cosmo-Localism and the Futures of Material Production.* https://actionforesight.net/cosmo-localism-and-the-futures-of-material-production/

List of Contributors

Jean-Francois Alesandrini is Senior Advisor, External Affairs and Executive Office at DNDi

Michel Bauwens is author and founder of the Foundation for Peer-to-Peer Alternatives

Cecile Blanchet is post-doc fellow at the German Research Centre for Geosciences

Sophie Bloemen is co-founder and director at Commons Network

David Bollier is director of the Reinventing the Commons Program at the Schumacher Center

Benjamin Coriat is professor of Economics at Paris 13 University

Sheila R. Foster is professor of Law and Public Policy at Georgetown University and co-director of LabGov

Thomas de Groot is Urban Policies and European Campaigns Lead at Commons Network

David Hammerstein is a public interest advocate, co-founder and senior advisor at Commons Network

Silke Helfrich is author and co-founder of Commons Strategies Group and of Das Commons-Institut

Ellen 't Hoen is senior researcher at UMC Global Health Unit of University of Groningen and director of Medicines Law and Policy

Christian Iaione is associate professor of Public Law at Guglielmo Marconi University of Rome, Fellow of the Urban Law Center at Fordham University and co-director of LabGov

Paul Keller is board member of Creative Commons and Europeana and co-founder of Communia

George Monbiot is an author, an activist and a columnist for The Guardian

Constantin Petcou is an architect and co-founder of atelier d'architecture autogérée

Doina Petrescu is professor of architecture and design activism at Sheffield University and co-founder of atelier d'architecture autogérée

Kate Raworth is an author and senior research associate at Oxford University and senior associate at the Cambridge Institure for Sustainability Leadership

Trebor Scholz is associate professor of culture and media at The New School in New York

Mai Ishikawa Sutton is a community organizer at People's Open Network, author and digital policy advocate

Alek Tarkowski is head of Centrum Cyfrowe, co-founder of Communia and Public Lead at Creative Commons in Poland

Mercè M. Tarrés is an artist, member of the Guerrilla Media Collective, and the illustrator of this book

Jose Luis Vivero Pol is regional analyst at the UN World Food Programme and research fellow at the University of Louvain

About the Editors

Sophie Bloemen, director and co-founder of Commons Network, is a political activist, author and policy advisor with a background in European political economy and philosophy.

Thomas de Groot, urban policies and campaigns lead at Commons Network, is a political activist, organisor and policy advisor with a background in Sinology, journalism and politics.